THE SANE ALTERNATIVE

THE SANE ALTERNATIVE

Signposts to a Self-fulfilling Future

James Robertson

1978

First published in 1978.
by James Robertson, 7 St. Ann's Villas, London W11 4RU
Copies can be obtained by mail from the above address.
Copyright © James Robertson, 1978

ISBN 0 9505962 0 5

Made and printed in Great Britain by Villiers Publications Ltd.,
Ingestre Road, London NW5 1UL

CONTENTS

ABOUT THE AUTHOR

James Robertson has been an independent writer, lecturer and consultant since 1973. He has worked mainly in Britain, USA, Canada, and France. Previously he had twenty years' experience in government, in management consultancy, and as research director for the British banks.

In the 1960s and early 1970s Robertson was a committed reformer — civil service, organisation of government, parliamentary procedures, the City of London as a financial centre, etc. In the last few years he has become increasingly convinced that, even if institutional reform were possible, it would not be enough. The crisis of modern society and the modern world goes much deeper.

James Robertson's previous books are listed on the back cover.

INTRODUCTION

The sane alternative will be self-fulfilling in two ways. It will be a future in which we fulfil ourselves, and develop our full potential as people. It will also be a future which comes about by its own momentum, once enough of us decide that it is possible and start to make it happen.

More and more people are feeling that in the next thirty or forty years the human race must break through to a new kind of future. Failure will mean disaster; success will mean an important upward step on the ladder of evolutionary progress. Many of us see this breakthrough as the central project, the historic task, for the two or three generations living at the present time — the task which gives meaning to our lives. We sense that a threefold era is now ending: first, the age which began with the industrial revolution two hundred years ago; second, the age of European ascendancy which began with the Renaissance and Reformation five hundred years ago; and, third, the age of the successor civilisations to Athens, Jerusalem, and Rome which began roughly with the birth of Christ two thousand years ago. This suggests a historical perspective, and a measure of our task as midwives to a new future.

Recognition that mankind is at a turning point is now fairly widespread. This book is not an attempt to provide original insights into its nature, nor to preach about it — whether to the converted or unconverted. Its purpose is to take the discussion on from there. It aims to meet a practical need.

I have become aware of this need in the last few years, while talking about our present situation and future possibilities with many people in Britain, Europe and North America. It is for a short and clear discussion document which will suggest:

what a sane, humane, ecological future will be like, as contrasted with other possible visions of the future;
by what kind of process of transformation that future

7

could evolve from the present, using momentum generated in the past;

what kind of activities will contribute to the successful achievement of this transformation.

I hope that three main types of reader will find the book useful.

First, there are people of the kind I have mentioned. They know that a new direction is necessary and possible for the future, and they want to help to steer things in that direction. The book may encourage some of them. It may help them to clarify some areas of thinking or decision — perhaps about their work or their lifestyle, or about how to discuss these questions with non-believers.

Second, the book is for people who do not feel such a high degree of personal commitment to the future, but who have a professional interest in the possibilities. These include industrial leaders, business managers, politicians, bankers, public administrators, trade unionists, academics, and members of professions like medicine, teaching and social work. Their activities will be profoundly affected by how the future evolves. They cannot ignore the prospect of the present being transformed into a sane, humane, ecological future. Increasingly, corporate planners, business forecasters, and public policy analysts are, in fact, studying and researching into future possibilities of this kind. The book may help to clarify their thinking. I hope it may also persuade some of them that the vision of the future outlined here, far from being utopian, may be more realistic and more feasible than any other alternative.

Third, the book is for people who, without as yet deep personal commitment or professional interest, want to start thinking more seriously about the future. Perhaps they have not yet wrestled with questions like 'Should we try to change ourselves first or society first?' and 'Should we discuss what we want the future to be, or what it will probably be?' (The answer — as to so many questions of this kind — is 'Some people should do one, some people should do the other, but most people should do both.') I hope that some of these readers will become interested in the possibilities for a sane, humane, ecological future and perhaps be encouraged to work for it.

8

The book has five main sections, as summarised below. Many readers will wish to read these straight through, one after another, from first to last. But each section can also stand on its own, as material for discussion in a group or class. As a whole, the book will provide preparatory reading material for five two-hour sessions at a weekend seminar, for a five-day course, or for a five-day module in a longer course (for example on management education). In other ways too I hope that groups of people meeting informally in one another's homes, as well as organisers of conferences, seminars, group discussions and training courses, will find the book contains something suitable for their purpose. Some questions for discussion are suggested at the end of each chapter, together with a short reading list.

It is especially important that questions about the future of society and the world should be discussed by groups containing all three types of reader I have mentioned. Activists with a strong personal commitment to a sane, humane, ecological future do not often have opportunities for serious discussions with professionals whose interest in the future is part of their job. Still less often do members of those two groups come together to discuss their different perspectives on the future with concerned but uncommitted laymen and women. Such tripartite discussion groups are not easily arranged as a matter of routine. Special arrangements are proposed in Chapter 5.

The five main sections of the book are as follows.

Chapter 1 discusses the choice of futures which seems to face us now, looking between thirty or forty years ahead. Five possibilities are considered: business-as-usual; disaster; the totalitarian conservationist (TC) future; the hyper-expansionist (HE) future; and the sane, humane, ecological (SHE) future. Objections to the first four are discussed. The chapter concludes with some reflections on the past as a source of insight for the future.

As an illustration of the change of direction involved in moving towards the SHE future, Chapter 2 discusses the present turning point in economics and economic activity. It describes the factors which are now beginning to limit further economic expansion of the kind we have taken for granted until recently. It suggests that the institutionalised, industrialised, technologically dominated economy of European origin — which developed from the Renaissance, through the Reformation and the industrial revolution and eventually spread over the whole world — is now overdeveloped to the point of breakdown. An equilibrium economy is contrasted with the conventional expansionist economy, and some features of the transition from expansionism to equilibrium are discussed. One of the most important features is identified as a shift of emphasis away from institutionalised economic activity (based on money and jobs) to personal, unstructured economic activity in households and local communities (where people provide themselves and one another with goods and services and care).

Chapter 2A may be of special interest to people in business, finance, trade unions and the economic departments of government. It adds to the discussion in Chapter 2 an analysis of the structural changes now taking place in the institutions of developed (or overdeveloped) economies. It suggests that these changes point towards a new principle of balance or equilibrium in economic institutions (economic democracy), which will be an important aspect of an equilibrium economy as described in Chapter 2. It also suggests that, as economic democracy develops further, it will encourage the de-institutionalisation of economic activity, again on the lines described in Chapter 2. It thus suggests that current changes in the institutional structure of the economy, introduced in response to pressures from the past, can be seen as potential steps towards a less institutionalised economy in the future. The breakdown of an old system of economic life and the breakthrough to a new one can be seen merging with one another in a single process of transformation.

Chapter 3 deals with 'paradigm shifts' as an aspect of transformation. It points out that changes in the meaning of wealth and growth will be part of the economic transformation discussed in Chapter 2. It suggests that similar changes in the meaning of power or health or knowledge will be part of a comparable transformation of politics, medicine and education. It discusses potential changes in the concept of work, as an aspect of transition from the industrial present to the SHE future. It points out that the encroachment of new ideas is a force for change, and that conscious metaphysical reconstruction is an important practical task.

Chapter 4 discusses some other aspects of the transformation. It points out that, not only in economics but in other spheres also, overdeveloped institutional and intellectual structures are an important part of the past that is breaking down, and personal and group experience and action are an important part of the future that should be encouraged to break through. Managing the breakdown of the old system can be seen as a task of decolonisation; creating the breakthrough to a new one can be seen as a task of liberation; and both can be seen as *enabling* people to be more fully themselves. Many different kinds of people have different roles to contribute to decolonisation and liberation, in helping to ensure that replacement of the old by the new is a peaceful process of evolutionary change. The transformation will be world-wide in scope, and the peoples of different countries will bring different perspectives to it. The chapter concludes by suggesting that psychological insights have a crucial part to play in coping with breakdown and breakthrough. Reference is made to psychotherapy; to the crises of adolescence and middle age which occur in the lives of individuals; and to transactional analysis (which considers people's relationships in terms of parents, children and adults) as a possible guide to development from dependence through independence to interdependence.

Chapter 5 is an aid, a guide and a stimulus to action. It re-affirms that the transformation of society will be brought about by a multitude of people doing their own thing. It suggests how a wide variety of transformation activities can be identified. It notes the need for a special kind of widely shared strategic thinking to map the way forward to the SHE future. It concludes with a summary list of proposals, including a specific project. An appendix contains the names and addresses of

11

people and organisations who may be able to give practical help, advice or information.

The book was written between January and August 1977 during a part-time attachment to the Department of Management Studies at Loughborough University of Technology. Early drafts of certain sections were discussed at seminars at Loughborough, and I am grateful to the participants for their helpful reactions and comments. I am particularly grateful to Gurth Higgin, Professor of Continuing Management Education at Loughborough, for arranging my attachment and the seminars there, and also for drawing my attention to recent work on the psycho-social factors which are relevant to the process of transformation with which the book is concerned.

I have other tangible debts to acknowledge. From March to June 1976 the Anglo German Foundation for the Study of Industrial Society commissioned me to carry out a part-time exploratory study on 'Policy Alternatives to Full Employment and Economic Growth'; this involved some preliminary work on alternative futures, on the nature of an equilibrium economy, and on the transition to it. A year later in the summer of 1977, The Stanford Research Institute invited me to write a *Guidelines* on 'Business Success in an Equilibrium Economy', which helped to clarify my thinking. Meanwhile, the International Foundation for Social Innovation in Paris had commissioned me to write a paper on 'Economic Democracy and Social Innovation' for their three-day meeting in March 1977. This provided an opportunity to work out the connection between economic democracy and economic equilibrium, and to speculate whether the transition to both might be a cumulative, self-sustaining process of psycho-social innovation, comparable to the self-sustaining economic and technical innovation which created the industrial revolution in eighteenth and nineteenth century Britain.

I also owe a debt of gratitude to many other people who have either discussed these questions with me personally, or have given me opportunities to discuss them with audiences large and small. Some of these people are mentioned at various places in the text. Three experiences have been especially valuable. One was travelling through the United States and Canada from August to October 1976, giving lectures and taking part in seminars with a wide variety of audiences, and meeting many people who — at the start of America's third century — were involved in one way or another in creating a better society. Another has been participation in the Turning Point network, which has provided links with a widening range of friends and correspondents, and is itself an example of the kind of shared activity that may be an important.element in the new future. The third has been the publication of my last two books, 'Profit Or People?' and 'Power, Money and Sex' by Marion Boyars in her excellent paperback series, Ideas in Progress. In these three contexts and in many others too, I am grateful to so many people for kindness and help and stimulus, and for new opportunities to learn.

Finally, there are three main reasons why I am publishing this book myself. I see self-publication as a modest but useful and interesting practical experiment in self-reliance — a venture in action learning — in keeping with the general message of the book. Second, I hope self-publication will enable me to encourage use of the book as discussion material, to assess its practical usefulness for that purpose, to revise it in response to suggestions, and to be in touch personally with people who find it useful. Third, self-publication will make the book an integral part of the project mentioned in Chapter 5. In this new venture of publication, as in the writing of the book, my greatest debt is to Alison Pritchard who has shared it with me throughout.

1
A Choice of Futures

Thinking about the future can be a complicated business. A recent guidebook[1]* to the literature on alternative futures contains reviews of over a thousand items. A recent report[2] on alternative futures for environmental policy in the United States described ten possible scenarios for the remaining years of the 20th century. It gave them names like 'hitting the jackpot', 'journey to transcendence', 'industrial renaissance', and 'mature calm'. Post-industrial society, super-industrial society, post-civilised society, technetronic society, convivial society, mature society, para-primitive society, psycho-social society, post-scarcity society, a learning and planning society — these are just a few of the ways that individual futurologists have described the particular kind of society they are predicting or recommending for the future. Think-tanks, policy research units, institutes for the future, professional futurists, computer models of the future — all these have proliferated during the last ten or fifteen years. If we had to discover and understand what they all think about the future, we should never begin to think about it for ourselves.

But we must think about it for ourselves. We can't just leave it to the experts. Experts tend to be narrow and specialised. This means that experts don't see the whole picture, and that different kinds of experts disagree about what is important. Experts make things complicated — either by mistake because they have forgotten how to think simply, or deliberately in order to impress us with their expertise. Experts — who, incidentally are usually men not women — always see the future as a reflection of themselves. If for the black writer James Baldwin 'the future is black', for the nuclear energy expert it is a nuclear energy future, and for the space expert it

---

* References are to be found in the bibliography at the end of the book.

is a future in which space travel and space colonisation are the key features. In general, if we leave the experts to think about the future for us, we thereby choose a certain kind of future —a future dominated by experts.

So we have to clarify things for ourselves. This means making some fairly simple starting assumptions. Mine are as follows.

(1) There are five distinctly different possibilities for the future, as discussed in this chapter.

(2) The next 30 or 40 years will be a critical period in the history of mankind.

(3) Thinking about the future is only useful and interesting if it affects what we do and how we live today.

(4) Practical thinking about the future involves a mixture of the following:
> predicting what is likely to happen,
> forecasting what would happen if . . . ,
> deciding what we want to happen,
> planning how to help it to happen;
> and acting accordingly.

Five Scenarios

Most people incline towards one or another of the following five views (or scenarios) of the future. Each one of the five is thought by some people to be the only realistic view. How do you feel about each of them? Which one do you prefer? Which do you think is likely to be closest to the actual future that will happen? I prefer the fifth, and this book is mainly about what it would be like, why it may come about, and how we can help to make it happen. The five views are as follows.

(1) *Business-As-Usual.* This view holds that the future will be much like the present and the past. There will no doubt continue to be many changes and crises, alarms and excursions, as there always have been. But the main problems of the industrial countries of Europe and North America, and of the world as a whole, will not change dramatically. Nor will the best methods of handling them. Nor will most people's general outlook and attitudes. This view can be presented as the only realistic approach to the practical problems of keeping things going in reasonably

16

good order. It appeals to placid and pragmatic people, good operators, successful trouble-shooters, moderate reformers, people who are content with their present position or their future prospects in the existing system. It also appeals to defeatists, cynics and worldly wisemen, critical of the present state of affairs but convinced they cannot change it and not prepared to try.

(2) *Disaster*. This view holds that things are beginning to break down catastrophically. There is no realistic alternative to nuclear war, and increasing unrest, famine, pollution, poverty, misery, disease and crime on a national and international scale. This view, too, can be presented as the only realistic view of the future. It is held by calm and thoughtful people, who have worked out the possibilities carefully, and who see no point in kidding themselves and others. It also attracts pessimists; hell-fire merchants, preachers and doomsters, who enjoy making other people uncomfortable and who like the limelight themselves; and people whose personal experience of failure has left its mark on their thinking about the world.

(3) *The Totalitarian Conservationist (TC) Future*. This view agrees with the previous one that the risk of disaster is very real, but holds that the best way to avert it is to accept an authoritarian system of government. People who hold this view point to the emergence of authoritarian regimes at previous crisis periods — Julius Caesar and Augustus after the collapse of the Roman Republic, Napoleon after the French Revolution, Hitler after the Weimar Republic in Germany, Stalin after the Russian Revolution — as evidence that people turn towards authority in times of chaos. They say that worldwide shortages and population pressures are creating a situation in which too many people are competing for too few resources. The only solution to this 'tragedy of the commons' (tc), in which uncontrolled individual greed destroys the common good, is a TC solution on the lines proposed by Hobbes in his 'Leviathan': we must give up our freedom to a sovereign power, which will enforce law and order and distribute the limited resources fairly to us

all; otherwise our lives will be poor, nasty, brutish and short. This view also can be presented persuasively as the only realistic approach to the future. It appeals to people who think they have more to lose from disorder than from dictatorship; to people of an authoritarian, dominating temperament; to people who take a low view of other people ('you can't change human nature'); and to people who think of themselves as belonging to the governing, rather than the governed, class.

(4) *The Hyper-expansionist (HE) Future.* This view holds that we can break out of our present problems by accelerating the super-industrialist drives in Western society, and in particular by making more effective use of science and technology. Space colonisation, nuclear power, computing, and genetic engineering can enable us to overcome the limits of geography, energy, intelligence and biology. This view appeals to optimistic, energetic, ambitious, competitive people for whom economic and technical achievement is more significant than personal and social growth. They are often male, and are likely to be toy-loving and over-cerebral. For many of today's opinion-formers, especially in Europe and North America, this is the only conceivable view of the future — and also an exciting one.

(5) *The Sane, Humane, Ecological (SHE) Future.* This view holds that, instead of accelerating, we should change direction: as I have said elsewhere,[3] the key to the future is not continuing expansion but balance — balance within ourselves, balance between ourselves and other people, balance between people and nature. Future expansion will be psychological and social; the important limits and the important frontiers now are social and psychological, not technical and economic. The only realistic course is to give top priority to learning to live supportively with one another on our small and crowded planet. This will involve decentralisation, not further centralisation. That is the only way of organising that will enable most people to fulfil themselves. We should aim to create a learning and planning society, a 'trans-industrial society' as Willis Harman[4] calls it. This view appeals to optimistic, partici-

pative, reflective people, who reject each of the first four views as unrealistic or unacceptable and believe that a better future is feasible. It is only fair to say that it also appeals to quite a large number of cranks.

Of these five views, Business-As-Usual is the only one which holds, in effect, that we do not need to concern ourselves much with the future; and Disaster is the only one which holds that catastrophe is inevitable. The last three share a serious concern about the future and a common belief that disaster is avoidable. But they disagree with one another about the most effective way of avoiding disaster; and they disagree about what kind of future is most desirable. TC recommends clampdown; HE recommends breakout; and SHE recommends breakthrough. TC and HE are elitist and centralist, while SHE is egalitarian and decentralist. HE and SHE are optimistic, while TC is pessimistic. TC and SHE are conservationist, while HE is expansionist.

We need to understand all these different views, because the actual future will almost certainly contain elements of all five: to some extent things will continue as before; to some extent there will be disasters; to some extent the enforcement of new regulations will be needed; to some extent new technologies will help us to break out of existing limits; and to some extent the evolution of new psychological and social capacities — at least in the form of better education — will be important. Although I prefer the fifth (SHE) view, I certainly don't deny that government and technology both have a positive contribution to make to a sane, humane, ecological world society.

Another reason for trying to understand all five views (and the differences between them) is that the actual future will be shaped by each interacting with the others. The dynamics of this kind of interaction are important. Other people approach the future differently from ourselves; only if we understand how and why, shall we know how to try to bring them over to our point of view; and, only by succeeding in that, shall we ensure that the actual future resembles the one we prefer.

So, with these points in mind, we now look a little more closely at each of the first four scenarios.

19

The Business-As-Usual Scenario

This scenario is taken for granted by most politicians, business leaders, trade union leaders, media commentators and members of other established institutions today. It is nowhere formulated very precisely. It has no articulate spokesmen. Those who subscribe to it assume, for practical purposes, that things will continue in the future much as they have in the past, and that that is all that needs to be said. So I will summarise it in my own words.

In political terms the Business-As-Usual scenario rests on three connected assumptions: that the nation state will remain the prime focus for political action; that representative politicians, political parties, a professional bureaucracy, and institutions representing industry, finance, trade unions and other interest groups, will continue to dominate the processes of politics and government; and that political choices will continue to be made within the broad ideological range of left, right and centre that has come to be taken for granted in the 19th and 20th centuries.

In the social sphere, the assumption is that social wellbeing will continue to depend largely on services provided by professional people and organisations — the main point of dispute being the conventional difference of opinion between left and right about whether these services should be paid for directly by their users, or whether they should be financed by taxation or some other form of public funding.

In the economic sphere, it is assumed that the mainspring of economic activity will continue to be manufacturing industry. Wealth will continue to be something which is created by the production and sale of goods, and consumed in the form of goods and services and amenities. The availability of good health, good education, and other forms of social wellbeing, will continue to depend on the prosperity of industries like automobile manufacturing, chemicals, and engineering. The prosperity of the developing countries will continue to depend quite largely on growing markets in the industrial countries. For all these reasons, the top priority will continue to be industrial productivity and economic growth. The main problems, it is assumed, will remain as they are at present. Political

20

debate will continue to centre on how much governments should intervene to secure high levels of industrial investment, high levels of employment and low levels of inflation, and to cushion the social and environmental impacts of industrialisation. There will continue to be a sharp distinction between the economic and social aspects of life, and between work and leisure, work and home. The 'work ethic' will remain strong, in the conventional sense that most men will continue to regard a job as a necessary prerequisite for status and self-esteem, while women identify more with the home and family.

This approach to the future has powerful attractions for many people. First, in terms of power and influence, the people who are well established in the present system of government, economics, social services and professional life, do not want to see it much changed. It is not easy for them to envisage what a different future would be like or how it would work. For example, in spite of growing doubts about the ability of the centralised nation state to handle either international problems or local matters, politicians and government officials find it hard to imagine any practical alternative focus for public affairs. Second, in the sphere of social welfare, people have become accustomed to depend on professional experts and organised services to provide their housing, education, medical treatment, and other forms of care. Many people would find it difficult to envisage an alternative. Third, in the economic sphere, most people (both in industrialised and developing countries) assume that material production, money and jobs are the essential goals of economic activity. The great majority of the world's population still aspire to greater material well-being and prosperity. The prospect of material growth has replaced religion as the opium of the people; and the richer and more influential citizens of every country in the world have a vested interest in its continuing credibility, since without it the demand for greater economic equality would be much stronger.

At the same time, the Business-As-Usual approach to the future ignores important questions. How can a world of nation states contain the arms race and the menace of nuclear war? How long can we continue with an asymmetrical economic

21

relationship between the industrial countries and the developing countries of the Third World — a relationship in which manufactured goods from the former are exchanged for raw materials and primary commodities from the latter? Are the industrialised countries already hitting physical, psychological, social and organisational limits to further economic growth? These are among the questions which other scenarios try to answer.

Disaster

The Disaster scenario has been articulated more clearly, for example by environmentalists and by campaigners for nuclear disarmament. According to Barry Commoner, many people respond to a recitation of the world's environmental problems with deep pessimism. He sees this as the natural aftermath to the shock of recognising that the vaunted 'progress' of modern civilisation is only a thin cloak for global catastrophe.[5] Commoner himself has expressed optimism; he feels that because the environmental crisis arises from our social actions, not from our biological needs, it can be resolved by bringing man's social organisation into harmony with the ecosphere. Paul Ehrlich is more doubtful. Like Barry Commoner, Ehrlich is a biologist. He agrees that, given the necessary changes in human attitude, we could successfully pull through the most dramatic crisis that mankind has faced. But he does not think such a change will occur. In 1969 Ehrlich said he 'would take even money that England will not exist in the year 2000, and give 10 to 1 that the life of the average Briton would be of distinctly lower quality than it is today.'[5]

The Club of Rome have also been concerned with the prospect of global disaster. Their first report, 'Limits To Growth',[6] had a tremendous impact on many people's thinking about the world's problems. Their second report, 'Mankind at the Turning Point',[7] was published by an international team of scientists and economists in 1975. It said, 'The rapid succession of crises which are currently engulfing the entire globe is the clearest indication that humanity is at a turning point in its historical evolution. The way to make doomsday prophecies self-fulfilling is to ignore the obvious signs of perils that lie ahead. Our scientifically conducted analysis of long term world development based on all available data points out quite clearly that such a passive course leads to disaster.' Meanwhile, Ronald Higgins in 'The Seventh Enemy'[8] had described the seven main threats to mankind's survival as:

Population Explosion
Food Shortage
Scarcity of Natural Resources
Pollution and Degradation of the Environment
Nuclear Energy
Uncontrolled Technology
Moral Blindness and Political Inertia.

In Higgins' view, 'We and our children are approaching a world of mounting confusion and horror. The next 25 years, possibly the next decade, will bring starvation to hundreds of millions, and hardship, disorder or war to most of the rest of us. Democracy, where it exists, has little chance of survival, nor in the longer run has our industrial way of life. There will not be a "better tomorrow" beyond our present troubles. That may sound hysterical. Yet it is what the evidence seen as a whole suggests.' Higgins' experience of economics, international diplomacy and central government had convinced him that, of his seven threats, the moral blindness of human beings and the painful inertia of our political institutions were what ultimately threatened disaster. The danger was that we would do too little too late to meet the other six threats, because this seventh enemy was too deeply entrenched.

Robert L. Heilbroner in 'An Enquiry Into The Human Prospect'[9] shared Ronald Higgins' despair. He concluded that a period of harsh adjustment was coming and he could see no realistic escape: 'If, then, by the question "Is there hope for man?" we ask whether it is possible to meet the challenges of the future without the payment of a fearful price, the answer must be: No, there is no such hope.' John Davoll, an author of 'A Blueprint for Survival',[10] is another whose analysis of the situation leads him towards the pessimism of Higgins and Heilbroner. Davoll is now the Director of the Conservation Society in Britain, and in the Society's annual report for 1976[11] he wrote, 'Although environmentalists have realised that a sustainable social and economic system would differ considerably from the existing one, they have usually taken it for granted that the transition from the old order to the new would be reasonably deliberate and orderly; the "Blueprint for Survival" in fact laid down a detailed timetable for the operation. Little attention was given to what political forces might propel this enterprise forward, and it seems to have been tacitly assumed that an intellectual conviction that mankind was heading for trouble, combined with a somewhat blurred vision of a more durable order, would suffice. Recent events have made it clear that anything like this is highly improbable. . . . The most probable outcome on the evidence of recent history, is, internally, the collapse of democracy into military rule and, externally, general warfare.'

It is difficult to argue convincingly against the likelihood of global disaster, as presented by thinkers like Heilbroner, Higgins and Davoll. The logic of their analysis points so clearly to it. Yet I find the pessimistic conclusion unacceptable on practical and moral grounds. We cannot allow ourselves to dwell on the prospect of disaster. We have to search for ways of avoiding it, whatever the odds against success, and that search — not prophecies of doom — should occupy our thinking and our energies. Moreover, the very threat of disaster may provide unexpected cause for hope. It might help us to mobilise the will and strength to achieve the apparently impossible. (It might also, on the other hand, destroy our morale.)

The next three scenarios offer three possibilities for avoiding catastrophe and creating a sustainable future. They are based on the totalitarian control (TC) approach, the hyper-expansionist (HE) approach, and the sane, humane, ecological (SHE) approach. Respectively they prescribe, as I have said, clampdown, breakout, and breakthrough.

Totalitarian Control
'People must be restrained, and the only question is how to go about achieving the necessary ends with the least odious and most effective means. . . . The rationale for world government with major coercive powers is overwhelming, raising the most

24

fundamental of all political questions: Who should rule, and how?' So writes William Ophuls in 'Leviathan or Oblivion'.[12] Although Ophuls mentions Aldous Huxley's 'Brave New World' as one possibility, he himself favours a return to the face-to-face life of small communities as a constituent part of planetary government. However, he says, 'only a sovereign would be strong enough to exact the sacrifices needed to return to the simple life.' Ophuls does not welcome the prospect of authoritarian government. He explicitly expresses antipathy to it. But he is among an increasing number of thinkers about the future of politics and government who see no alternative.

In considering the prospect of a future in which control by authoritarian government would play a central part, we have to consider who wants it, how likely it is, and whether it would work if it came about.

Very few people admit that they would welcome this kind of future. But there are quite a lot who undoubtedly would. Superior, censorious, insecure people like to see other people kept in their place. Among the professional, business, financial and bureaucratic middle classes in the countries of North America and Western and Eastern Europe today there are many who fear the prospect of disorder more than they fear the prospect of neo-fascism or neo-stalinism. In times of uncertainty there will always be many members of the police and military forces ready to impose law and order with a firm hand. So, although I don't want a TC future myself (which is one reason why I think it so important to work for a viable future of a different kind), I realise that there are many people who would welcome it.

A realistic view must put the likelihood of a TC future quite high — as thinkers like Ophuls do. Centralised authoritarian control could fairly easily encroach as a natural and painless, indeed necessary, development from the rather muddled kind of corporate state that has been evolving in countries like Britain since the second world war, and from the expanding role of government in countries like the United States. There are, as I have said, many people who would welcome it, and many others who would be prepared to accept it as the only practical alternative to disaster if law and order began to

25

collapse. If we are to avoid a TC future, we have to recognise that its probability is quite high, and we have to understand the viewpoint of people who would welcome it or accept it.

The third question is crucially important: would a TC future actually work? It is often taken for granted that authoritarian government would be effective, although perhaps undesirable. This seems to be assumed especially by North American thinkers who have never experienced how muddled and inefficient centralised bureaucratic government actually is. I won't repeat what I said about this in 'Power, Money and Sex'. But the evidence suggests that, the more totalitarian they are, the more the 'proliferative and self-serving character of almost all known bureaucracies' (John Davoll) is compounded with incompetence. There is virtually no hard evidence — only wishful thinking — to suggest that authoritarian government (or more regulations than we have in countries like Britain today) would provide effective means to surmount the crises of the next thirty or forty years.

Thus the TC scenario is unacceptable on two counts: it would be nasty; and it wouldn't work.

The two remaining alternatives — the HE future and the SHE future — are based on the view that, instead of clamping down, we should seek to break out or break through. They both stand towards the TC philosophy much as the uncontrolled expansionist philosophies of John Locke and Adam Smith stood towards the authoritarian restrictionist philosophy of Hobbes. They are both concerned not so much with the protection and allocation of the limited space and resources already available, as with the creation of new space and new resources — physical and economic in the one case, psychological and social in the other. Both are more positive and optimistic than the TC approach. But the directions which they envisage for the future are diametrically opposed.

The Hyper-Expansionist (HE) Future

Exponents of this view include Herman Kahn[13] and Daniel Bell.[14] It holds that the human race, having expanded over every part of planet Earth since the 15th century, is now poised to colonise space; that scientific knowledge, having advanced ever more rapidly since the 16th and 17th centuries, is now about to capture the commanding heights of biology, psychology, communication and control; and that industrialism, having developed a dominating economic role since the 18th and 19th centuries, is now bringing super-industrial society to birth. A splendid future now beckons Western, scientific, industrial man if only he has the courage of his convictions.

Kahn believes that we are now at the mid-point of a 400-year period that began 200 years ago with the industrial revolution. 'We have just seen in the most advanced countries the initial emergence of super-industrial economies (where enterprises are extraordinarily large, encompassing and pervasive forces in both the physical and societal environments), to be followed soon by post-industrial economies (where the task of producing the necessities of life has become trivially easy because of technological advancement and economic development). We expect that almost all countries eventually will develop the characteristics of super- and post-industrial societies.' For the more immediate future Kahn believes that 'barring extreme mismanagement or bad luck, the period 1976-1985 should be characterised by the highest average rate of world economic growth in history.' In general, he presents what he calls 'a plausible scenario for a "growth" world that leads not to disaster but to prosperity and plenty.'

Bell specifies the following five components of what he calls post-industrial society:

(1) Economic sector: the change from a goods-producing to a service economy;
(2) Occupational distribution: the pre-eminence of the professional and technical class;
(3) Axial principle: the centrality of theoretical knowledge as the source of innovation and of policy formulation for the society;
(4) Future orientation: the control of technology and technology assessment;
(5) Decision making: the creation of a new intellectual technology.

The Hyper-Expansionist or super-industrial future is thus

27

seen as a logical extension of the industrial past. Just as the economies of today's industrial countries progressed historically from the primary commodity stage to the secondary manufacturing stage, so now they are progressing through the tertiary service stage towards the quaternary service-to-service stage. Among the growing points in an economy of this kind are universities, research institutes and consultancies, and industries like aerospace, telecommunications and computing. All these provide services to sectors like transport, communications and finance, which themselves provide services to corporations and individuals. Shifting the emphasis into these knowledge-based, high technology industries and services will, according to this scenario, enable today's industrial countries to retain their markets in the developing countries as the latter enter fully on the industrial manufacturing stage.

The Hyper-Expansionist scenario shares the underlying assumptions of the Business-As-Usual scenario, that 'wealth' is created by the provision and sale of goods and services which other people and other countries will be willing to buy, and that expansion can continue indefinitely. The prospect of space colonisation is an important element in it. So is the further development of nuclear power as an energy source. The Hyper-Expansionist scenario shares the Business-As-Usual scenario's assumption that the economic relationship between the industrialised and developing countries will continue to be asymmetrical, with the former continuing to lead the latter along the path of economic progress. But the Hyper-Expansionist scenario is more challenging than the Business-As-Usual scenario. It holds that the future for today's industrialised countries lies in accelerating the shift from conventional manufacturing industry to the high technology, know-how, and professional service industries; and that the underlying task for the business system (and for public policy) in those countries is to manage this transition successfully.

This scenario conforms to the widespread assumption that progress means increasing technical sophistication and the extrapolation of existing trends. But it also raises many unsolved questions — technical, political, and psychological. The feasibility of widespread automation, space colonisation, and massive nuclear power programmes in the next few decades is not assured. When the basic needs of billions of third world people are not yet met, will it be possible for the industrialised countries to concentrate on creating a high technology future? In the industrialised countries themselves transitional unemployment would be very high. Society would be polarised beween a comparatively small number of experts and technocrats on the one hand and the leisured irresponsible masses on the other. Even if it did prove possible to make the transition to that kind of society, would it satisfy the higher level needs of most people for self-esteem and self-fulfilment? It is not at all clear how the hyper-expansionist approach would break out of the limits which (as we shall see) seem now to be closing in on the developed economies of today.

It is sometimes assumed that the HE future is the only possible post-industrial future. But, as Michael Marien has shown (in a recent paper* as yet unpublished), there have for many years been two conflicting meanings of 'post-industrial' and two completely different visions of post-industrial society. Marien describes the first as the vision of a technological, affluent, service society, and the second as the vision of a decentralised, agrarian economy following in the wake of the failure of industrialism. As thus described, the second gives too negative an impression of what I call the SHE view of the future. But I entirely agree with Marien that the two opposing views of post-industrial society will be focal points for ideological debate in the coming decades.

To sum up, I do not personally find the HE quite as nasty as the TC scenario, though it is exploitative, elitist and unsympathetic. But, in my view, it is not feasible for the reasons I have suggested. This leaves us with the SHE scenario. Later chapters will discuss different aspects of it and how it can be achieved. The rest of this chapter discusses what insights about it can be gained by looking back into the past.

A Choice of Pasts

The fall of the Roman Empire is often quoted as a turning point in history that is comparable to the present time. Heilbroner[15] is one of those who holds the view that mankind is

* Now see *Futures*, October 1977, pp.415-431.

now entering a new dark age. He pessimistically likens our present prospects to the Roman Empire's period of decline in the 5th and 6th centuries AD, when 'the established institutions of the Empire gradually lost their ability to cope with the orderly provision of the former Roman territories, and in which a deep and pervasive crisis of faith, simultaneously destroyed the Empire from within.' William Irwin Thompson[16] makes the same comparison between that period and this, but he sees the dark ages as creative periods. He instances the 6th century Christian monastery school of Lindisfarne (on Holy Island, Northumberland, England) as an example of a small, short-lived community creating new light and revitalising old philosophies against a background of darkness and destruction. In establishing a contemporary Lindisfarne Institute in New York, Thompson and his colleagues 'have gone back on the spiral to the pre-industrial community to create, on a higher plane with the most advanced scientific and spiritual thought we can achieve, the planetary, meta-industrial village. . . . We are trying to create an educational community that can become a mutational deme in which cultural evolution can move from civilisation to planetisation.' L. S. Stavrianos, in 'The Promise of the Coming Dark Age',[17] also looks on the Dark Age following the collapse of Rome as an age of epochal creativity, when values and institutions were evolved that constitute the bedrock foundation of modern civilisation. The Dark Age was an age of birth as well as of death, a dynamic and seminal phase in human history. Stavrianos points out that the present shares four important features with that period — economic imperialism, ecological degradation, bureaucratic ossification and a flight from reason. But these parallels between the two periods lead Stavrianos to an optimistic and constructive view of the future. He sees it in terms of a movement from aristo-technology to demo-technology, from boss control to worker control, from representative democracy to participatory democracy, and from self-subordination to self-actualisation.

Thus, looking back to the fall of the Roman Empire may throw some light on the possibilities for our future today.

But there is a more telling approach. If we do indeed stand at the beginning of a new future, then we must also be standing

30

at the end of an old past. What is this past that we are leaving? The more clearly we identify it and the better we understand its nature, the more clearly we shall understand the future upon which we are now entering.

Are we, then, coming to the end of a 200 year period in history — the period which was shaped by the emergence of representative political democracy in the American and French revolutions and by the industrial revolution? Does this mean we should look forward to post-representative politics and a post-industrial revolution? Murray Bookchin[18] is among those who look back 200 years for a period comparable to the present time. He finds it in the revolutionary Enlightenment that swept through France in the 18th century — a period which, as he says, completely reworked French consciousness and prepared the conditions for the Great Revolution of 1789. A disintegrating social process was taking place in which the ancient regime lost credibility, in which a vast critique of the old system developed, and in which more and more people began spontaneously to withdraw their support from it. Bookchin feels that the same thing is happening today, but it is a century and a half of embourgeoisement that is now breaking down and bourgeois institutions that are collapsing. Other people, like Daniel Bell, have put forward the idea of a post-industrial revolution as today's counterpart to the industrial revolution. We have mentioned this idea already, and we shall examine later the possibility of a new breakthrough in psychological and social development which would compare with the economic and technical breakthrough of 200 years ago.

But there is another possibility. For the beginning of the era which is now passing, perhaps we should be looking back not 200 years but 500. Are we now coming to the end of the individualist, masculine, rational, scientific, expansionist, European period of history which began with the Renaissance and the Reformation? Should we be looking forward now to a less individualistic, more feminine, post-scientific, post-European era?

Three changes which mark the transition from the Middle Ages to modern times seem to have particular relevance for us today. The first was the shift from the religious outlook of the

Middle Ages to the political and economic values of the post-Reformation age. The second was the growing need people felt in the 15th and 16th centuries to liberate themselves from the domination of mediaeval institutions, especially the Church, which prevented a sense of personal contact with reality. The third was the growing artificiality and incredibility of the traditional intellectual framework — the theological structure elaborated by the schoolmen — which ultimately led to its collapse. All of these have important parallels today.

R. H. Tawney in 'Religion and the Rise of Capitalism'[19] described how the theological mould which shaped political theory in the Middle Ages was broken at the Renaissance. Machiavelli emancipated the state from religion; politics became a science; reason took the place of revelation; and the basis for political institutions became expedience, not religious authority. Somewhat later an objective and passionless economic science also emerged. Thus politics and economics became self-contained departments of life in their own right, and religion was relegated to a self-contained department of its own. More recently, Gurth Higgin[20] has also described how the 'social project' of mediaeval society was religion. Beliefs about reality, sanctions for social order, and the reasons behind all activities, were directly derived from religion. Adherence to them was seen as serving religion. This did not mean that everyone was religious all the time. But it did mean that most people were concerned with their religious condition; that, as the mediaeval cathedrals testify, the Church was the dominant institution of society; and that theology was the queen of the sciences. Then 'the settled religious social project of the Middle Ages began to lose its power, and — in spite of a bitter and vigorous rearguard action — its leading part, the Church, also finally suffered decline. Western European societies were developing a new social project, a social project that replaced religious by economic values. . . . Whereas in the Middle Ages the most heinous crimes were blasphemy, heresy, witchcraft and other crimes against religion, in the new order the most serious crimes are those against property and in particular its symbol, money.'

Higgin goes on to compare that transition from the Middle

Ages to modern times with the transition we are entering upon today. He suggests that it is now the turn of the economic 'social project' to wither, and along with it its 'leading social part' (manufacturing industry) and its 'leading psychological part' (an alienating willingness to dedicate one's life to being merely an instrument of work). 'The name of the game in the Middle Ages was religion. The name of the game in the industrial era is economics. What it might be in the more distant future nobody knows.'

My guess is that the new name of the game will be the development of shared consciousness; and that religion, politics and economics will come together again in this single vision of the meaning of life.

The Renaissance and the Reformation brought about personal liberation and the collapse of the old conceptual framework by stressing the value of individual experience and observation at the expense of received doctrine and authority. The religious symbolism of mediaeval art gave way to human realism, and eventually artists like Leonardo relied almost entirely on study and experiment as the best guide to the truth, not on tradition and convention. Luther argued that the Christian needed no elaborate paraphernalia of religious ceremonies and ecclesiastical institutions to teach him his duty or to correct him if he neglected it: let him listen to the scriptures and his own conscience. Luther felt that to externalise religion in rules and ordinances was to degrade it. The Bible was translated out of Latin into languages that people could understand.

Today a similarly compelling desire to make closer personal contact with reality is widely felt. It shows itself as a growing interest in decentralised energy systems — solar panels, windmills, etc. — which put individuals and households more directly in touch with natural energy sources; as a desire to grow more of our own food and to do more things for ourselves, and thus to be more directly in touch with the materials and natural resources on which we depend; and as an urge to develop our own capacities for spiritual experience and explore our own consciousness, rather than being content with the ceremonies and doctrines of formal religion as mediated to us by priests. In general, it shows itself in a growing desire to liberate ourselves from the institutional and intellectual structures of modern society which have become buffers between ourselves and what we feel is real.

Meanwhile, the highly specialised mumbo-jumbo of economists and social scientists seems less and less relevant to real needs. 'New generations of researchers are inculcated with an orthodox vision elaborated with more and more concrete details. The increasing amount of empirical findings accumulated and organised within the given conceptual framework requires an increased effort on the part of the individual who would learn the state of the field. It also creates more questions than it settles and tends,therefore,to lead to increasing specialisation. When this happens it becomes more and more difficult for the individual to avoid scientific myopia, and to keep his subject in perspective and maintain a dispassionate overview of the entire field. In particular, it becomes difficult to keep in mind that alternative, latent visions, capable of organising the same collections of "facts", must always exist — or to imagine what these alternatives would be.'[21] Are economists and social scientists now performing the role which the schoolmen performed in the dying Middle Ages? Are the economic and social sciences losing credibility as a guide to action, just as theology lost credibility in the 15th and 16th centuries?

But perhaps 500 years is not enough. Perhaps, in order to understand what age is now ending for us, we should look back 2000 years to the beginning of the era which took its character from the Hebrew, Greek and Roman civilisations. Astrologers call it the Age of Pisces and say that the Age of Aquarius is now beginning. Most of us think of it as the Christian era. Will the future age be the age of a post-Christian planetary culture?

There are certainly some interesting parallels between the situation now and that which existed 2000 years ago. For example, Jewish religious law had become formalised and fossilised, like our overdeveloped institutions today. It was 'forgotten that the Law was designed as an aid to rectitude, not as an end in itself. Correct observance was so manifold and took up so much time that the majority of simpler souls had pardonably arrived at the tacit conclusion that such outward obedience was all that mattered. Prayer, probity, charity, and moral soundness in general had become regarded as a species of tax payable to the deity, rather than a means of communion with the deity. The ideal, organic relationship between man and god was threatening to turn into just such a fortuitous and inconsequential one as characterised the pagan creeds. Abstract monotheism too had become very much externalised. This state of affairs was what Jesus set out to remedy.'[22]

Second, just as Roman imperialism and administration had then created conditions for the mediterranean world in which Christianity could spread and flourish, so today European imperialism and modern technologies of transport and communication have created conditions favourable to the spread of a single planetary culture. As Jesus, John and Paul then brought together the spiritual, intellectual and organising genius of the Hebrew, Greek and Roman traditions to create the foundations for a new world religion and civilisation, so today various strands seem to be converging — for example, from ecology, from Eastern mysticism, from humanistic psychology and from the Christianity of Teilhard de Chardin — to create a new planetary movement from which a new civilisation may spring. As the early spread of Christianity took off, so perhaps we should now be prepared for a new world movement to blossom and spread. In the early Christian movement martyrdom was of the essence, following the example of Christ; and part of the combat training of the early Christians was to discuss the sufferings and deaths of their martyred friends in order to prepare themselves to endure similar torture and humiliation when their time came. Will non-violence be the central principle of action in the new planetary movement that is in prospect now? Will an important feature of the new movement be the sharing of experience of non-violent action, and the training of one another for it?

So, industrial revolution, Renaissance and Reformation, the beginning of the Christian era — which of these should we regard as the beginning of the age which is now ending? From which can we learn the most relevant insights about the future which we face today? The answer must be all three. The old structure has become institutionalised and sterile; conditions have been created in which a new movement, capturing new energies, can spread and flourish; the new movement will be based on the urge to break through to more direct contact and communion with reality; the new movement will become self-sustaining in ways that owe comparatively little to the dominant mechanisms and motivating drives of the age that is passing. These features of the historical watersheds of 200, 500, and 2000 years ago are features of our situation today. They tell us something about the nature of the post-industrial, post-European, post-Christian future — the sane, humane, ecological future — which is now beginning; and they give us some ideas about the nature of the transition to it.

Suggested Questions for Discussion

1. Do you think that the five scenarios — Business-As-Usual, Disaster, TC, HE and SHE — cover all the possibilities? Or are there any others, which are just as important?
2. Do you agree that what Ronald Higgins calls the seventh enemy is the most important of the threats facing mankind? Or are there others equally important?
3. Do you agree with Michael Marien that there are two quite distinct, indeed opposing, visions of post-industrial society? Which do you prefer?
4. What part do you think expert futurologists should play in helping people to assess future possibilities and in helping them to work for the kind of future they would like?

Suggested Reading

Michael Marien[1] is an immensely valuable guidebook to over 1000 different books and papers about the future.
Robin Clarke[5] is an interesting collection of papers by 24 different writers.
Ronald Higgins[8] ⎱ provide convincing arguments
Robert Heilbroner[9] ⎰ for the Disaster scenario.
Herman E. Daly[12] contains contributions by Garrett Hardin and William Ophuls dealing with the TC scenario.

Herman Kahn[13]
Daniel Bell[14] } put forward the HE scenario.

James Robertson[3]
Willis Harman[4] } put forward the SHE scenario.

References are to be found in the bibliography at the end of the book.

2
A Prodigal's Return:
Economics Prepares To Come Home

A 'decline of business civilisation' is taking place, says Robert Heilbroner.[15] George C. Lodge[23] says that a 'new ideology' is emerging which will transform the relationship between business and society. Others say that economic democracy is now beginning to take its place alongside the kind of political democracy which originated with the American and French Revolutions 200 years ago. Yet others say that economic activity, having emerged as a separate department of life since the Renaissance and the Reformation, is now converging again with the social and political domains. E. F. Schumacher[24] says we have to rethink economics, 'as if people mattered'.

This chapter discusses some key features of the present situation and some of the prospects it holds out. First, we shall consider the limits to further economic expansion which are now beginning to close in. Second, we shall look at what an equilibrium economy would be like, in contrast to an expansionist economy. Third, we shall examine the prospects for a less institutionalised economy, i.e. an economy which is less dependent on money and jobs than today's industrialised economies, and which puts greater emphasis on activities in and around households and local communities. The insights we gain from this are also relevant to politics, knowledge, religion and other important spheres of life, as well as to economics. In all of them we shall find, for example, that over-developed institutional and intellectual structures are part of the past that is breaking down, and that personal experience and action are part of the future that we want to encourage to break through.

Limits to Economic Expansion
(1) Physical Limits

The fixed dimensions and finite resources of planet Earth cannot allow economic growth to continue indefinitely. This general hypothesis has been increasingly accepted as common sense since the publication of 'Limits To Growth'[6] in 1972, in spite of economists' counter attacks and technical criticisms from other academics and scientists. As Emile Benoit has pointed out, the thinking of classical economists such as J. S. Mill about a 'stationary state' of economic activity has now been integrated with the insights of ecology and the imagery of the space age — for example by Kenneth Boulding in 'The Economics of The Coming Spaceship Earth'.[12] Benoit[25] summarises the new situation as follows: 'Our earth, we now begin to realise, does not and cannot supply us with an unlimited amount of usable energy, raw materials, foodstuffs, safe dumping grounds for our waste products — or even standing room. It is not an inexhaustible cornucopia. It is much more like an inter-planetary vehicle, where resources must be carefully conserved, waste products must be minimised and recycled, and where the number of passengers must be carefully limited to those that can be taken aboard without overcrowding . . . We have, in effect, a revolution of rising expectation, superimposed on a population explosion, in a world of fixed dimensions and limited productive capacity. Therein lies the problem.'

Technical arguments about how soon the planet's resources will run out, and about how soon this strictly physical limit will be reached, have been heated and complicated in recent years. For practical purposes it is sensible to assume that, combined with the other limits discussed below, potential shortages of available energy and resources will compel mankind to adopt a permanently sustainable pattern of economic activity within 30 to 40 years, say by the year 2015, if we are to avoid catastrophic disasters.

(2) Social Scarcity

As Fred Hirsch has pointed out in 'Social Limits to Growth',[26] the expansion of the institutionalised economy tends to decrease the value of socially scarce goods once they are attained. He cites traffic congestion and higher education as examples. The satisfaction derived from an automobile depends on the traffic conditions in which it can be used, and these will deteriorate as use becomes more widespread. The competitive value of higher education, as a launching pad for a good job, goes down as the number of highly educated people goes up; as access to higher education spreads, its 'positional' value declines. Hirsch contrasts the positional economy with what he calls the material economy in which what one person enjoys does not reduce the value of what other people enjoy. He defines the positional economy as covering everything that is either scarce in itself or subject to congestion by extensive use; and he points out that, 'as general standards of living rise . . . competition moves increasingly from the material sector to the positional sector, where what one wins another loses in a zero-sum game. As the frontier closes, positional competition intensifies . . . In the positional sector, individuals chase each other's tails. The race gets longer for the same prize.'

In other words, many of the goods delivered by the institutionalised economy become progressively less valuable as it grows. Eventually a limit is reached. The advanced industrial countries are not far off it now, in many respects.

(3) Psychological Remoteness

As more and more people in an industrialised society come to depend for more and more aspects of their life on remote, impersonal institutions, rather than on their own efforts and the efforts of people they live with in the household and local community, their sense of alienation and dependence grows greater. They therefore feel entitled — indeed, compelled — to make greater and greater demands on the economy for jobs, for pay, for goods and commercial services, and for public and social services. Sooner or later the time is bound to come when these demands will outrun the economy's capacity to meet them. At this point the economy becomes locked into a combination of rising unemployment (too big a demand for jobs) and rising inflation (too big a demand for money); there is then no way the institutionalised economy can develop which will not make matters worse. In 1976 Peter Jay, until recently Economic Editor of *The Times*, and now British Ambassador in the United States, described this situation as 'the contradiction of existing political economy.'[27] He reached 'the depressing conclusion that the operation of free democcracy appears to force governments into positions (the commitment to full employment) which prevent them from taking the steps (fiscal and monetary restraint) which are necessary to arrest the menace (accelerating inflation) that threatens to undermine the condition (stable prosperity) on which political stability and therefore liberal democracy depend. In other words, democracy has itself by the tail and is eating itself up fast.'

(4) Institutional Congestion

As the institutionalised economy has developed, it has inevitably become increasingly complex and congested. It has now reached the point where the supposedly wealth-creating activities of industry and commerce are generating such great social costs, and the interrelations between industry, finance, government, trade unions, and the public services have become so intertwined, that the workings of the system are grinding towards a halt. The American economist, Hazel Henderson, describes this as 'the entropy state' which, she says, 'is a society at the stage when complexity and interdependence have reached such unmodelable, unmanageable proportions that its transaction costs equal or exceed its productive capabilities. In a manner analogous to physical systems, the society winds down of its own weight and the proportion of its gross national product that must be spent in mediating conflicts, controlling crime, footing the bill for all the social costs generated by the externalities of production and consumption, providing ever more comprehensive bureaucratic co-ordination, and generally trying to maintain "social homeostasis", begins to grow exponentially or even hyper-exponentially. Such societies may have already drifted to a soft-landing in a steady state, with inflation masking their declining condition.'[28]

(5) Conceptual Disarray

The conventionally accepted intellectual framework for understanding how the economy works — the prevailing paradigm of modern economic life — is beginning to lose credibility.

For example, the idea that economic wealth is something that must be created by industry and commerce before it can be spent on the provision of social wellbeing by the public

41

services is wearing thin. Increasingly, people are asking why it should be necessary to build and sell more automobiles in order to be able to afford more schools and teachers; or why it should be necessary to make and sell more cigarettes and sweets in order to be able to afford more doctors and dentists. They are asking: what sort of 'wealth' is this, which is created and consumed in this way? and they are increasingly coming up with answers like the following: 'To the indiscriminate growth economists it doesn't matter whether the products of industrial activity are more sweets to rot the children's teeth, or insulating blocks for houses. Essentially, the concern is with measured economic busyness rather than with purposes.'[29]

Again, the idea that wealth, or national product, is created only by activity in the money-based, institutional sector of the economy and not by activity in the informal domestic and local community sector — for example, that the economic production of the country actually goes down if people grow their own vegetables instead of buying them in the shops — is also wearing thin. As Hugh Stretton has put it in 'Housing and Government', 'How easily we could turn the tables on the economists if we all decided that from tomorrow morning, the work of the domestic economy should be paid for. Instead of cooking dinner for her own lot, each housewife would feed her neighbors at regular restaurant rates; then they'd cook for her family and get their money back. We'd do each other's housework and gardening at award rates. Big money would change hands when we fixed each other's tap washers and electric plugs at the plumbers' and electricians' rates. Without a scrap of extra work Gross National Product (GNP) would go up by a third overnight. We would increase that to half if the children rented each other's back yards and paid each other as play supervisors, and we could double it if we all went to bed next door at regular massage parlor rates. Our economists would immediately be eager to find out what line of investment was showing such fabulous growth in capital/output ratio. They'd find that housing was bettered only by double beds and they'd recommend a massive switch of investment into both. Don't laugh, because in reverse, this

42

nonsense measures exactly the distortion we get in our national accounts now.'[30]

Economists are, in fact, increasingly beginning to claim that GNP has never purported to measure the "use value" of economic activity; they have always recognised that it simply represents the "exchange value" of all goods and services produced in the money economy; it does not differentiate between desirable and undesirable economic activity; nor does it differentiate between final economic consumption and intermediate economic activity which is undertaken to treat disease, clean up pollution, salvage accidents and mitigate damage caused by other economic activities. Some analysts are actually suggesting that rising GNP in industrialised countries now measures mainly the rising costs of pollution, environmental degradation and human suffering; and although that cannot be proved, it is a further indication of the declining credibility of rising GNP either as a measure of economic wellbeing or as a desirable goal of economic endeavour.

(6) Summing Up

There is thus a whole variety of ways in which the thrust of conventional economic activity is bumping against limits. This applies to the world economy as a whole, but in particular to the industrialised countries. Different people emphasise the importance of different limits. But in general it is becoming clear that a change of direction will have to take place, towards *economic equilibrium* instead of economic expansion, and towards economic *de-institutionalisation* instead of further economic institutionalisation.

Towards An Equilibrium Economy

An equilibrium economy will be an essential part of the SHE future. I shall not attempt to draw up a blueprint. I shall simply try to convey a sense of the changes that will be required in the world economy today, and in particular in the industrialised countries, if we are to move towards economic equilibrium. The need is to identify some of the practical consequences of these impending changes — not only as they will affect us as men and women with our personal lives to live, but also as they will affect us in our more specialised roles as

43

business people, doctors, planners, politicians, government officials, trade unionists, bankers, public servants, teachers, and so on. But, first, two general points.

An equilibrium economy would not involve returning to pre-industrial conditions, with poverty and subsistence farming as the prevailing mode of life. This is sometimes alleged by people who cannot conceive an acceptable alternative to perpetual economic expansion. The truth is that by moving towards an equilibrium economy, based on sane, humane, ecological use of advanced technology, mankind will have a better chance of meeting economic needs and achieving a high quality of life, than by trying to prolong the conventional trajectory of economic growth.

The second point is this. Many conservationists stress the physical limits to further economic expansion, but are less aware of the social, psychological, institutional and conceptual limits. They tend to assume that authoritarian controls will be needed — and will be able — to impose economic equilibrium. In Chapter 1, in the context of the TC scenario, we saw reason to doubt the capability of authoritarian governments to do this successfully. Here we question the need. As the limits to economic growth continue to press more heavily, it is quite likely that more and more people whose basic material needs are secure will slacken off. They will relax, not intensify, competition with one another for unnecessary economic and material advantage, preferring to concentrate on achieving psychological rewards and social goals. Psychological and social growth will take priority over the economic, materialist rat-race. There is, in fact, evidence that this may be happening already. A survey carried out in April 1977 for 'New Society'[31] reported that the British have become 'remarkably unambitious in a material sense. Very few sincerely want to be rich. Most people in Britain neither want nor expect a great deal more money. Even if they could get it, the vast majority do not seem prepared to work harder for it: most respondents thought they should only work as much as they needed to live a pleasant life. What's more the British seem to have lowered their sights since 1973. . . . There appears to be a new phenomenon: a revolution of falling expectations.'

44

The following would be among the most important features of an equilibrium economy. Try to imagine what they might mean for your way of life and work.

(1) *Energy and Resources*

An equilibrium economy would reflect the principles of ecology. Mankind's use of resources would reflect the way resources are used in nature. The economic system would become an integral part of the larger ecological system, i.e. a closed loop of material cycles powered by the sun.

In making the transition to an equilibrium economy we should, as Kenneth Boulding[12] says, be leaving the open 'cowboy' economy of the past in which mankind was able to exploit the apparently limitless spaces and resources of an under-populated planet, and entering a closed 'spaceman' economy in which the earth has become 'a single spaceship without unlimited reservoirs of anything either for extraction or for pollution, and in which therefore man must find his place in a cyclical ecological system.'

Like any well-managed enterprise an equilibrium economy would use income, not capital, to meet its recurrent needs. It would depend on renewable energy supplies from sun or wind or water or natural vegetation, and not on exhaustible once-for-all deposits of fossil fuels. Manufacturing industry would process and reprocess renewable and recyclable materials, rather than convert unrenewable and exhaustible materials into products which are later thrown away as waste. Agricultural production similarly would become a self-sustaining process in which renewable sources of fertility would be used as a perpetual source of income, rather than a once-for-all process of using up physical capital (in the form of natural soil fertility, and of chemical fertilisers and pesticides derived from fossil fuels and other exhaustible mineral deposits).

(2) *Lower Throughput, Greater Durability*

Compared with today's pattern of economic activity in the industrial countries, an equilibrium economy would place greater emphasis on the durability of manufactured products. Repair and maintenance and servicing would be relatively more important than they are today. What people need in order to enjoy a high quality of life would be more clearly distinguished

45

from what they could be persuaded to want by advertising and promotional techniques.

(3) *People First, Things Second*

The industrial economy of the last 200 years has focussed primarily on things. As consumers people have become accustomed to want more things, and as workers they have become accustomed to subordinate themselves to the requirements of factories, machines, and assembly lines. In the equilibrium economy the production and distribution of things would become a relatively less important part of the economy than the provision of services, care and amenity for people; and even the processes of producing and distributing things would become more people-orientated. Already in modern economies employment has been shifting from manufacturing to services, and participation and job satisfaction have been attracting increasing concern.

A people-orientated equilibrium economy would rely more heavily on the energies and skills of people than the industrial or hyper-expansionist economies. This does not mean going back to the bad old days of labour-intensive drudgery. It means that people's energies and skills would be recognised as an important renewable resource, as contrasted with the unrenewable energy and materials required to make and operate capital-intensive plant; and it means that satisfying and rewarding occupation would be an important economic objective in itself. In the industrial economy the employment of people has represented a cost which employers aimed to reduce. In an equilibrium economy, it is the reduction of opportunities for personally satisfying and socially useful occupation that would be regarded as a cost; high priority would be given to developing the activities, the technologies and the kind of organisations required to make such opportunities widely available. In terms of Abraham Maslow's[32] hierarchy of needs, a growth economy has concentrated on meeting people's physiological needs and need for safety, whereas the emphasis in an equilibrium economy would shift towards also meeting people's higher level needs for belongingness and love, esteem, and self-actualisation.

(4)   *Greater Self-Sufficiency*

The industrial economy has been based on the idea that progress involves greater and greater economic specialisation, differentiation and interdependence. The hyper-expansionist view of the future not only accepts this idea, but argues for accelerated progress of this kind, for example in areas like knowledge, leisure and personal care. The equilibrium economy, while recognising that some degree of specialisation is valuable, would also recognise that there are desirable limits to it and that in many respects those limits have been exceeded. In practice, therefore, the transition to an equilibrium economy would put more emphasis on self-sufficiency than on further specialisation.

As a general rule, each country, each region, each district, each locality and each household would aim to be rather more self-sufficient economically, and rather less dependent, than is the case in the world economy and in the industrialised countries' economies today. For example, there would be a prevailing tendency to try to be more self-sufficient in food production and energy, and to be less dependent on traded commodities and traded manufactures. This would involve development for today's neglected pockets in the industrialised countries, as it would for the poor countries. The long-term impact on international, as well as internal, patterns of trade and investment would be important. The present asymmetry of economic relationships between industrialised and developing countries would be reduced. This would be consistent with current Third World demands for a new international economic order.

Various factors would encourage this tendency towards greater self-sufficiency. First, income energy from the sun and income resources generated by continuing natural processes like plant growth tend to be more widely dispersed than deposits of fossil fuels and minerals. Second, the less developed countries will become increasingly reluctant to exchange their primary commodities for manufactured goods. Third, the costs of transport may continue to rise quite sharply, with rising energy costs. Fourth, the psychological appeal of greater self-sufficiency is likely to become stronger, as people come to see it both as a

47

way to reduce their sense of economic insecurity and dependence, and as a way of getting closer to nature and reality.

(5)   *A More Decentralised Economy*

Pressures for economic decentralisation are already evident in most of the industrialised countries in Western Europe and North America. So are pressures for political devolution. Increasingly, these two approaches to decentralisation are likely to interact, to converge and to become mutually reinforcing. In Britain, for example, it will be surprising if assemblies with political powers in Scotland and Wales do not try to reverse the recent trend to greater and greater concentration (larger and larger firms) in British industry. In an equilibrium economy, characterised by a greater degree of self-sufficiency at every level than exists today, the pressures to decentralise would be reinforced. The focus for business activity could be expected to shift from national business corporations (and, in some countries, nationalised industries) towards a more locally based business system. And, in government, a reversal could be expected of the trend in recent years towards increasingly centralised management of national economies.

It seems unlikely that, in general, we shall see a worldwide return to traditional entrepreneurial, small scale, private capitalism. Political realities seem to point in the opposite direction in most industrial countries. Most probably, business decentralisation will take a variety of forms. In large enterprises, we may expect to see the interests of all the main stakeholders (employees, investors, customers and the public) represented in decision-making at national, regional and local levels — the guiding principle being to maintain a balance between these interests rather than to optimise any one of them. But there will also be greater scope than there is today for small businesses of all kinds — privately owned, worker-owned, community owned, self-employed, and so forth.

The changing institutional structure of the economy is discussed in greater detail in Chapter 2A.

(6)   *The International Economy*

The Business-As-Usual and the HE scenarios would involve increasing international specialisation and the continuance of asymmetrical economic relationships between industrialised and Third World countries. Conversely, the achievement of an equilibrium world economy, whose constituent parts were more self-sufficient and more decentralised, would involve convergence between the economies of industrialised countries and Third World countries.

During the transition to equilibrium, international economic activity would be harnessed to the common objective of helping each region and country to become more self-sufficient. This would involve a more truly international approach to world economic development than at present, including in many instances the transfer of know-how and experience from Third World countries to the overdeveloped countries.

(7) *Appropriate Technology*

An important feature of an equilibrium economy will be a shift of emphasis from big technology, as in today's industrial and hyper-industrial economies, to the development of advanced technologies of an appropriate form and scale. More effort will go into designing and producing machines and systems for individuals and small communities to use. These will be specifically aimed at helping people to meet more of their own household or local needs in spheres such as food and agriculture, building, repairs and maintenance of all kinds, leisure and entertainment, and also energy and transport. More generally, the idea that technology can be appropriate or inappropriate will have a much greater influence than it does today — the idea being that technology ought to be good to work with, sparing in its use of resources, produce a good end product, and be kind to the environment.

The idea that capital-intensive technology is appropriate for the advanced countries and intermediate technology for the developing countries will not apply in an equilibrium world economy.

(8) *Town And Country*

In an equilibrium economy, more self-sufficient and less centralised than today, worldwide urbanisation will have slowed and will probably have been reversed.

This may have started to happen already in North America and Western Europe. The cost of feeding, housing, maintaining and providing heat, light, power and transport for people in

49

cities is continuing to rise. The problem of providing satisfying employment and useful occupation for people in cities is growing worse. The trend towards megalopolis may already have reached its limit in cities like Tokyo, London and New York.

As we move towards economic equilibrium a sizeable rural resettlement movement is likely to emerge, with increasing emphasis on part-time farming and on the rejuvenation of rural communities. This will be consistent with more self-sufficiency and decentralisation, and in conflict with the further development of agribusiness farming. Space will become available in city centres for more convivial ways of life than industrialised society has permitted or than the HE scenario would allow. Millions of people will change their patterns of travel, transport, communication, shopping and entertainment.

(9) *Greater Economic Equality*

Assuming the levels of education and personal liberty now prevailing in the western industrial democracies, an equilibrium economy will necessarily be more equal than most economies today. In an expansionist economy inequalities of resource consumption can be justified by the argument that they motivate the abler members of society to create more wealth for all: he who makes the cake bigger can be rewarded with a bigger slice for himself. In an equilibrium economy that argument will not apply; there will be more resentment against inequalities on the part of the disadvantaged, and a lesser degree of commitment to them on the part of the privileged.

In an equilibrium world economy the poorer countries will press for greater equality than today. When the world economy was expanding it may not have mattered very much that the average North American used twice as much energy as the average European, and the average European six times as much as the average inhabitant of the developing countries. But an equilibrium economy will not tolerate such differences in resource consumption. Rectifying them will obviously mean big changes, with simpler and more frugal lifestyles for most North Americans and Europeans.

These changes will be partly effected in today's industrial countries by switching to durability instead of throughput, recycling instead of throwing away, effective utilisation instead

50

of waste. Much could be achieved in this way without reducing standards of living or quality of life at all. Going beyond mere conservation, an equilibrium economy will also depend on the spread of voluntary simplicity — a sense that using an ever increasing share of the planet's resources is not the most rewarding way to live, even from one's own point of view.

(10) *Work, Leisure and Life*

The contrast between the HE and SHE scenarios is particularly revealing here. In the HE scenario leisure becomes an important professionalised industry. As people acquire more leisure and more money, the leisure market grows and the leisure industry becomes larger and more sophisticated. The split between work and leisure that characterises the industrial economy is accentuated in the hyper-expansionist economy.

By contrast, without going back to pre-industrial conditions, the equilibrium economy of the SHE scenario will blur the split between work and leisure. More people will live nearer to their work than in industrialised societies today, and their work will also be more closely integrated with other aspects of their lives. The boundaries between work and family, work and the local community, work and leisure, and paid work and unpaid work (like housework), will be less clear cut than in the industrial and hyper-industrial economies. More people will spend more of their time working in the informal sector of the economy where money is not the main measure of value. Fewer people will spend as much time as people spend today working for an employer in the labour market.

In an equilibrium economy people will be less willing to work at jobs which they perceive as personally frustrating or socially or ecologically damaging or futile; they will insist on spending their working time in ways that contribute to social wellbeing and their own self-actualisation. Men and women will share more equally the paid work they do for other people and the unpaid work they do for themselves, their families and their friends. The economic role of the family and the local community will acquire a new importance. The dividing line between economic and social activities and between economic and social policies — which has become increasingly sharp in the industrialised growth economy — will tend to fade. And

51

that brings us, nicely and neatly, to the future of the dual economy.

The Dual Economy: A Reversal of Past Trends

I have suggested that overdeveloped institutional and intellectual structures are an important part of what is breaking down, and that personal experience and action are an important part of what should be encouraged to break through. A good example of overdeveloped structure is the institutionalised economy based on money and jobs, and a good example of personal experience and action is the informal (gift and barter) economy* of households and local communities. I have suggested that the institutionalised economy has reached the limits of its development in the industrialised countries. I have also suggested that in an equilibrium economy the boundaries between work and family, work and the local community, work and leisure, paid work and unpaid work, will be less clear cut than they have become in modern industrial societies. The prospect of a change of direction in the development of the dual economy is clearly on the cards.

Figure 1 shows the economy divided into two parts. The insitutionalised part is shown above the horizontal line, the informal part below it.

The *institutionalised part* of the economy is the part in which people work for money in jobs generated by the labour market; the goods they make and the services they provide are purchased for money or otherwise financed, for example by taxation. This part of the economy consists of the primary (farming, forestry, mining) sector, the secondary (manufacturing) sector, and the tertiary and quaternary (services and service-to-services) sectors. The *informal part* of the economy consists of the domestic (household) sector and the marginal (community) sector. In this part of the economy the labour market does not operate (people don't have jobs), work is mainly unpaid (like housework), and goods and services are mainly given away or exchanged. The informal part of the

---

* I acknowledge a debt here to Peter Cadogan's[44] concept of the 'gift economy'.

THE DUAL ECONOMY

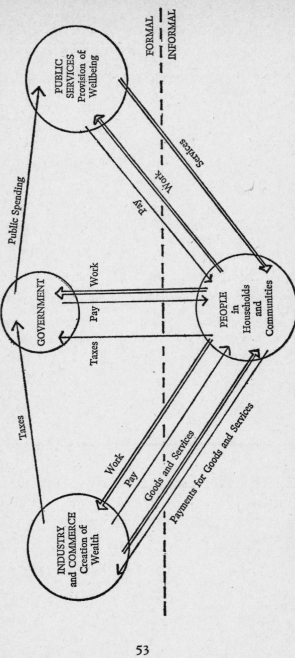

FIGURE 1

economy is sometimes described as the gift and barter economy, as opposed to the money economy, though it also includes many unrecorded cash transactions.

Everyone lives, to a greater or lesser extent, in both parts of the dual economy. But in industrialised societies attention is concentrated on the institutional part of the economy, the part in which business corporations, government agencies and other organisations operate and in which individuals make and spend money. The prevailing concept of wealth is of something created in the institutionalised part of the economy by the 'economic' activities of industry and commerce and then spent, partly on the consumption of goods and services which people purchase from industry and commerce, and partly on the provision of 'social' wellbeing by public services. These public services are financed as a spin-off from the economic activities of industry and commerce, which are therefore seen as the 'wealth-creating' activities of society.

It is no doubt true that representatives of established opinion in the industrialised countries — conservatives and liberals — capitalists and socialists — spokesmen for business, finance and trade unions — politicians, government officials, commentators in the news media, private lobbies and public interest groups — hold differing opinions about how the economy should work, and about what changes should be made in various aspects of it. But they all share the prevailing assumption that the production of economic goods and the provision of social services by the institutionalised part of the economy are the only kinds of economic activity that really matter. Economists and statisticians, politicians and civil servants, trade unionists and bankers, are concerned only with the kind of goods and services which cost money and with the kind of work which is done for an employer — jobs in the so-called labour market. Work which is done in the household or marginal sectors, such as housework, does not count in the employment statistics; and goods which are produced there, such as fruit and vegetables grown in gardens and allotments, do not count in the Gross National Product (GNP).

The thrust of industrialisation, and the momentum it has developed in the past 200 years, has driven people increasingly

out of the informal part of the economy into the institutionalised part. The pressure continues today. For example, single-
parent mothers and fathers are encouraged to go out of their
homes into jobs in the labour market, thus making the children
dependent on institutionalised child care services. In general,
men, women and children alike are encouraged to look outside
the home for work, for the physical necessities of life, for
teaching, for care, for entertainment. The process has been
self-reinforcing, like the drift from public transport to private
transport. As economic activity has shifted away from the home
and local community, the home and local community have
become less and less able to meet the economic and social
needs of the people who still remain there, thus pushing them
also into the money economy, the labour market and the
organised social services. We have never stopped to ask whether
we would all be better off if we lived a greater proportion of
our lives in the informal economy. We have never tried to find
the right balance between the two halves of the dual economy.

But now economics is preparing to come home. I believe that
an important feature of the post-industrial revolution will be
a reversal of the hitherto prevailing shift out of informal into
formal economic activity. More people will decide to spend a
greater part of their time in the informal economy. They will
find ways of reducing, rather than increasing, their dependence
on money, jobs and social services provided by the institutionalised economy. There are some signs of this beginning to
happen already in countries like Britain and the United States.

So what kind of a process will this be, this reversal of institutionalisation in the economy? I believe it will have two main
aspects, reinforcing one another. One aspect is that people will
liberate themselves — to a greater or lesser extent — from
dependence on the institutionalised economy; they will develop
their own alternative forms of economic activity in the informal
economy. They will decide to do more of their work and more
of their living in and around their households and local communities — to create use value rather than exchange value by
their work. As more and more people decide to do this, they
will create a growing movement towards greater economic self-
reliance, alternative technologies, alternative health, rural

55

resettlement, and so on. The other aspect is that people in responsible positions in the institutionalised economy will encourage its de-institutionalisation. People who work in the big organisations of government, business, finance, trade unions, public services, and the professions will increasingly see their role as helping other people (as well as themselves) to reduce their dependence on jobs, on money and on goods and services provided by industry, commerce, government and the public services. Increasingly they will aim to enable people — as citizens, customers, workers, patients, pupils and so on — to develop their own autonomy. In thus helping others to liberate themselves, they will *decolonise* the institutionalised economy.

One of the most important aspects of the transition to the SHE future will be a programme for economic liberation and decolonisation on these lines. We shall discuss its practicalities in Chapters 4 and 5.

Suggested Questions for Discussion

1. Do you agree that the industrialised countries are now hitting limits to economic expansion. Do you think that these limits are already causing a revolution of falling material aspirations — a movement towards voluntary simplicity?

2. Which of the ten features of an equilibrium economy do you think is the most important? and which do you think most people would find the most difficult to accept?

3. Do you think a more labour-intensive (people-intensive) economy, in which there was more work for people to do, would be better or worse than the capital-intensive (machine-intensive) economies of Europe and North America today?

4. In which half of the dual economy, formal or informal, do you think you personally spend too much (or too little) time and energy? Or is your life well-balanced in this respect? Why do you like (or dislike) the idea that men naturally work in the formal, and women in the

informal, half of the economy?

5. Have you ever seriously tried to reduce your dependence on money, on your job, and on social and public services? What could you do, if you wanted to, to liberate yourself from the institutionalised economy in this way? Have you ever seriously tried to help other people to liberate themselves from the institutionalised economy? What could you do in this respect if you decided to try?

Suggested Reading

Schumacher[24] Heilbroner[15] Daly[12] Lodge[23]	are recommended for the general reader.
Hirsch[26] Jay[27]	are recommended for the reader who is particularly interested in economics.

2A
The Meaning of Economic Democracy

Chapter 2 described several different ways in which the accepted economic systems of the industrialised countries are bumping against limits, and are beginning to break down. It suggested that we now have to do two interconnected things: we have to move towards an equilibrium economy; and we have to reverse the institutionalisation of economic activity.

Readers who are heavily engaged in what are commonly thought to be the pressing issues of practical economy today — multinational companies, the European Economic Community, industrial democracy, prices and incomes policy, investment in industry, for example — may not have found it easy to relate the ideas in Chapter 2 directly to their own existing preoccupations. This second part of Chapter 2 discusses recent developments that may seem more relevant to readers of that kind. (Some other readers may find this chapter less interesting, and are invited to skip it, if they so wish.) It shows that the institutional structure of the developed economies has become unsettled and out of balance; that current structural changes in economic institutions can be seen as leading towards a new balance between the various groups of participants in economic activity; that this new balance can be described as economic democracy; and that the concept of economic democracy applies at every level from the United Nations to the individual household. It also suggests that this new democratic balance will be an important feature of an equilibrium economy; and that, as it develops in the formal part of the economy, it is also likely to encourage a new balance between the formal and informal parts. This second part of Chapter 2 thus suggests that changes which are now being made in the structure of economic institutions in response to pressures arising from the past can be seen as fore-runners to the kind of changes in economic activity which are needed to meet the needs of the future.

The simplified model of a national economic system shown in Figure 2 is based on British institutions. But it illustrates interactions and relationships which apply in all industrialised countries. We can study how an economic system is evolving by looking at how these relationships are changing. We can draw comparisons between the economic systems of different countries by noting how the various relationships differ from one country to another.

Starting with the business enterprise, I have described elsewhere[33] how a business enterprise of any kind — whether it be a shareholder company, a public corporation, a worker co-operative or a consumer co-operative — will be related to four main types of stakeholder. These are its customers, its employees, its investors and the public. Formal relations between the enterprise and its stakeholders are articulated by the systems of Law and Money. The law lays down the rights and obligations between the stakeholders, and the flows of money between them embody many of these rights and obligations. As Figure 2 shows, these flows of money include payments from the enterprise to its employees (wages, salaries, etc.), to its investors (dividends and interest) and to the government (taxes and rates); and payments to the company from customers (for goods and services purchased), from investors (new capital), and from the government (investment incentives and subsidies). Relations between a business enterprise and its stakeholders will, of course, be determined not only by formal considerations of law and money but also by its informal attitudes and theirs. The attitudes of an enterprise and the business policies arising from them will be shaped by the directors and management, the directors theoretically being responsible for making policy and management being responsible for carrying it out.

At the level of the enterprise, economic democracy is concerned with the representation of the stakeholders' interests, with the resolution of conflicts between them, with the accountability of directors and managers to the stakeholders, and with procedures for making decisions about the enterprise's policies and actions, including decisions affecting the

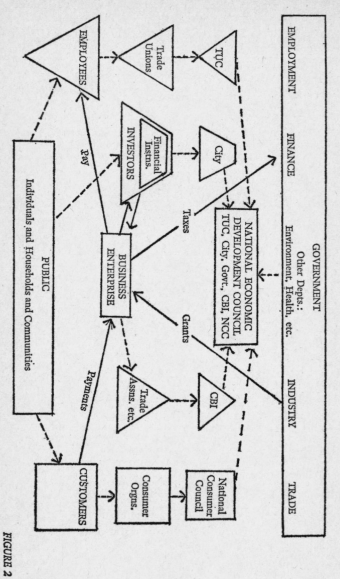

GOVERNMENT AND THE ECONOMY

EMPLOYEES

Trade Unions

TUC

INVESTORS
Financial Instns.

City

Pay

Taxes

NATIONAL ECONOMIC
DEVELOPMENT COUNCIL
TUC, City, Govt., CBI, NCC

PUBLIC
Individuals and Households and Communities

BUSINESS
ENTERPRISE

Grants

Trade Assns. etc.

CBI

Payments

CUSTOMERS

Consumer Orgns.

National Consumer Council

GOVERNMENT

EMPLOYMENT

FINANCE

Other Depts.:
Environment, Health, etc.

INDUSTRY

TRADE

FIGURE 2

60

distribution of financial benefits and financial costs between the various classes of stakeholder. An enormous amount of discussion and study of these questions has been taking place in all the industrialised countries in recent years — participation, industrial democracy, co-determination, social responsibilities, accounting and reporting procedures, profit sharing, improving the availability of investment finance, corporate taxation strategy, government incentives for industrial investment, and so on. Much of this discussion and study is now on an international basis.

Standing behind the four main stakeholders (customers, employees, investors, and the public) and also behind the directors and management, are various institutions which play a crucial part in the working of an economic system. Behind the customers there stand consumer organisations and a National Consumer Council, whose function is to support the customer interest. Behind the employees are the trade unions and the Trade Union Congress (TUC), whose function is to represent the employee interest. Individual investors in companies are being steadily replaced by financial institutions (pension funds, insurance companies, etc.) whose function is to represent the financial interest of all the individuals whose pension contributions, insurance policies, etc. they hold in trust; and the City of London and the Bank of England represent the investor interest at the national level. Standing behind the individual business enterprise are trade associations and employers' associations, backed at the national level by the Confederation of British Industries (CBI); and standing behind the directors and the management are the Institute of Directors and the British Institute of Management. Finally, central and local government stands behind the public to represent and safeguard the multiple interests of the public in the enterprise and in the business system generally.

The changing roles of trade unions, financial institutions, the government, the CBI, and — to a lesser extent — the consumer organisations, have been among the most important changes in Britain's economic system during the last thirty years. We discuss them in the following section. In one sense these changes can be seen as a movement towards a centralised

61

corporate state. But they can also be seen as a movement towards economic democracy.

The role of government in the economic system is, of course, crucial. As shown in Figure 2, it concerns itself with the role of the business system in relation to such aspects of the national interest as the environment, health, and so on. Through its economic departments it concerns itself with employment, finance, and trade, as well as with the general wellbeing of the country's industrial system. Governments legislate specifically to protect employees, investors and customers and the public, and to regulate the relationships between them and the enterprises in which they have a stake; and many government agencies have now come into existence in every country to administer legislation in these fields. More generally, for many governments today one of the most important functions in relation to the business system is economic planning and industrial planning. A department of industry may legislate to this end; and in many countries there is a planning organisation — in Britain the National Economic Development Council (NEDC) is an example — in which representatives of government, industry, trade unions, the financial institutions and the consumer organisations participate in economic planning and policy making. In some countries, notably France, the introduction of national economic planning has probably been among the most important developments in the economic system in the last thirty years.

The manner in which these various economic institutions interrelate, and the power which they exercise, differs greatly from one country to another. Some countries have centralised economic systems, in the sense that the main economic decisions are taken centrally, while others have decentralised economic systems in the sense that individual enterprises have a great deal of freedom to pursue their own policies. Some economic systems are predominantly capitalist, in the sense that the investor interest is paramount; others are predominantly socialist, in the sense that state ownership and control is paramount; in others, as in Yugoslavia, worker-managed enterprises predominate; theoretically, other economic systems might be dominated by municipal or consumer enterprises (i.e.

by businesses owned by the local community or by their customers); and many countries have a 'mixed economy', containing a mixture of these various types of enterprise.

The institutional balance of a country's economic system, as outlined in the previous paragraph, will tend to coincide with the dominant ideology in that country. However, the pressure of events will tend to produce changes in the institutional structure ahead of changes in the ideology. Thus a country like the United States with a Lockean ideology based on individual enterprise and property rights may fail to recognise the extent to which its economic system has become dominated by big business corporations; and a country like Britain which prides itself on having an open 'mixed economy' may fail to recognise how far it has developed in the direction of a centralised corporate state. The types of economic system which we define as market capitalism (or social market economy), corporate statism, state socialism (or state capitalism), and the various decentralised forms of socialism (in which enterprises are controlled by their workers, their consumers, or the local public), all represent different ideologies. The 'mixed economy' (which has now become a 'muddled economy') appears to represent an ideology in transition and confused.

The dynamic of this interaction between the evolution of economic systems and the evolution of ideologies is important. When it becomes recognised that a country's economic system has developed in ways divergent from the conventionally prevailing ideology, both the economic system and the ideology are exposed to question: is the new economic system acceptable? is the old ideology still valid? This means that, as new structures of economic democracy continue to emerge to meet the needs of the times in various countries of the world, they are likely to be influenced by, as well as to influence, the emerging ideologies of the future. If a new planetary ideology is indeed emerging, based on an ethic of ecology, social responsibility, and self-realisation, we should expect that this will soon help to shape the newly emerging structures of economic democracy.

Changes in Britain's economic system in the last half century are a good example of the kind of structural changes which are occurring in all the industrialised countries. Every element in the system shown in Figure 2 has been involved.

First, there has been increasing concentration in the business system itself.[34] In 1935 half of the manufacturing sector's output was produced by the 800 biggest companies, in 1958 by the 420 biggest, in 1970 by the 140 biggest, and the merger mania of the early 'seventies has further increased this process of concentration.

Second, and equally important, has been the increasing concentration of power in other economic institutions outside the business system, i.e. in government, trade unions and finance, and the drift towards a centralised corporate state.

Government. A greater proportion of British business than ever before is now directly controlled by government — nationalised either by deliberate policy or as the only way to rescue otherwise bankrupt industries. Other forms of government intervention in the business system have grown continually too. Legislation protecting employees, investors, consumers and the public, and also legislation aimed at making industry more efficient, now hedges the business enterprise on all sides. Through the 1960s and the 1970s the government has continually increased its financial help to industry — the high technology industries like aerospace and computers no less than older industries in difficulty like shipbuilding and motorcars. Government intervention to restructure industry by promoting mergers has grown greatly. Since 1960 continuing government efforts have been made in various ways to develop machinery and procedures for economic and industrial planning, and for prices and incomes control, in consultation with industry, the trade unions and finance.

Trade Unions. The trade unions have also been growing bigger and more powerful. Between 1960 and 1974 the number of unions with 100,000 members or more grew from 17 to 25, and their total membership from $6\frac{1}{2}$ million to $9\frac{1}{4}$ million, while the total number of unions dropped from 664 to 488. It is true that the trade union movement in Britain is still very fragmented, compared with certain other countries like Germany. But the statistics tell only part of the story. The successful development of collective bargaining has led to greater and greater participation in economic decision-making by the trade union movement at every level. The 1974 Labour Government's 'social contract' with the trade unions has been central to its economic policy. Since then the trade unions have participated fully in formulating industrial strategy in the NEDC. In 1977 the Bullock Committee[35] on Industrial Democracy advocated a comparable extension of trade union power in the individual firm.

Financial Institutions. The financial institutions, similarly, have been growing bigger and more powerful. The figures show that personal shareholdings in large companies dropped significantly between 1963 and 1975, while the holdings of institutions (insurance companies, pension funds, banks, nominee companies, and charities and non-profit bodies) rose correspondingly. As the Diamond Royal Commission[36] put it, 'What seems to have been happening is that individuals as a group have been turning away from direct investment in industry and placing their savings with pension funds, life insurance companies, unit trusts, etc., which in turn invest them in industry.' So far as personal control over investment decisions is concerned, this change can be seen as as move away from economic democracy. It clearly raises questions about the social responsibilities and democratic accountability of the comparatively small number of fund managers who now control the investment decisions and financial policies of the big shareholding institutions. On the other hand, the concentration of financial control, like concentration of trade union power and concentration in the business system itself, should make it easier for the elected government to evolve and carry out an effective industrial strategy at the national level. Thus in one sense these developments can be perceived as a move towards economic democracy, at least in principle.

All in all, the growing power of government, of the trade unions and of financial institutions has eroded the power of business leaders to direct and manage. Business managements are now hedged in by a jungle of legislation, and by the possibility of intervention in their affairs by government, trade unions, and (perhaps to a lesser extent) the financial institutions. Thus the authority of business managements has been much weakened. But at the same time, paradoxically, business leaders have become part of a governing economic elite in which they share national economic power with trade union leaders, financial leaders and government.

The dynamics of social change are such that, as one would have expected, this drift towards a corporate state has been followed by a grassroots backlash, arising from the steadily growing awareness of small people, including small business enterprises, that they are now too much dominated by the big battalions. It may be true in one sense, that the politicisation of economic decision making at the national level is a step towards economic democracy. But if it involves increasingly centralised economic power, where does that leave democracy? Decentralisation has now become the most pressing item on the agenda for economic democracy.

Third, while these changes have been taking place in the environment of the business enterprise, big changes have been taking place in the internal structure and ethos of the enterprise itself.

> For example, systems of decentralised management have been introduced in many firms, as they have become larger. Most successful large enterprises have by now developed effective principles and practice of decentralised control. Could these lead smoothly to democratic decentralisation and even, in the future, to the total break-up of many of today's big companies?

> Again, much effort has been put into schemes of employee participation (and more recently industrial democracy and co-determination), sometimes accompanied by the introduction of profit sharing schemes; and also into the practicalities of social responsibility in business, sometimes leading to the introduction of internal social audit.

66

These reforms in employee participation and social accountability can be seen cynically as defensive moves by business managements to stave off growing demands for more effective economic democracy. But they can also be interpreted as steps towards the internalisation of social controls — a new social balance — in the economic enterprise.

Yet again, our perceptions of the management role have been changing. Professor John Morris[37] of the Manchester Business School has sketched changes that have taken place in the prevailing paradigm of the business manager, first as the executive agent of the shareholders, next as the leader of a joint enterprise, and now as the balancer (or arbiter) between the multiple interests of the various stakeholders. As new structures of economic democracy emerge, we should envisage further changes in the prevailing managerial paradigm. As we shall see in Chapter 4, the concept of the manager as an enabler (or decoloniser) will become increasingly important from now on.

Much effort has been and is being spent on all these internal aspects of change in the business enterprise by business experts of all kinds, including industrial relations experts. Even if much of it is still being done in a fairly narrow perspective — as a belated defence against the assaults of business competition, trade union power and public interest pressures — it is preparing the ground for a different future.

To sum up. Until quite recently all these changes in the structure of British economic institutions could be seen as a process of continuing adjustment to meet new pressures as they arose, to correct malfunctions as they became apparent, and to respond to the changes in the balance of economic power as they made themselves felt. The outside observer would have recognised that particular features of the British system — the City of London or the trade union movement perhaps — created special pressures for change or presented special obstacles to it; and he would have noticed British delegations to other countries seeking helpful insights for handling particular aspects of economic and industrial affairs — to Sweden for incomes policy, to France for economic planning, to Japan for industrial innovation, to Germany for industrial financing, and so on. But he would almost certainly have assumed that the purpose and result of this process of continual adjustment and change was simply to maintain the essential institutional structure of the mixed economy. It is only quite recently that it has become clear that the kind of political economy that now exists in Britain and the other industrialised democracies is inherently unstable.

Some International Comparisons

In the two previous sections we have briefly outlined a general institutional model of the economy in an industrialised country, and the kind of changes that have been taking place in the structure of one country's economic institutions in recent years. But various features of the economic system, and various ways in which the system is changing, differ from country to country. To understand how economic democracy is likely to emerge in one country as compared with others we need to understand these differences.

For example, take the trade unions. In Britain the trade unions are socialist in ideology and in politics they are allied with one of the two governing parties. They have recently been the government's partners in the 'social contract', deeply involved in economic policy at national and sectoral levels. But (partly because of the multiplicity of trade unions) they have retained the traditional adversary conception of their role within the enterprise. Hence the opposition from many trade unionists to the Bullock Committee's proposals for worker representation on company boards, and the insistence by others that such representation should be no more than an extension of collective bargaining. In short, current thinking about economic democracy in Britain tends to be dominated by the position of the trade unions, and is confused because they are undecided between their adversary and partner roles.

In the United States, on the other hand, the trade unions are robustly capitalist — adversaries to management only in the sense of wanting a bigger share of the fruits of the capitalist system. There is no question of the trade unions partnering a socialist government, because state socialism is anathema in the United States. So current pressures for economic democracy in the United States are coming not from the trade unions but from the minority group, environmental and consumerist lobbies like Nader's raiders, and from what Peter Drucker[38] has recently described as pension fund socialism. 'Social responsibility' has been the big challenge to management in the United States, 'participation' in Britain.

Now take the financial institutions. In Britain and the United States they are based on financial markets like the Stock Exchange, though in Britain the big banks and other financial institutions are becoming more dominant than they were. In both these countries people working in the financial sector are concerned primarily with the management of money (i.e. making money out of money) rather than with the management of industry. In Germany, on the other hand, the financial sector is dominated by the big banks, which are much more concerned than in Britain and the United States with the successful management of industry. In France the financial sector is dominated by banks and other financial institutions as in Germany, but the most important institutions are nationalised. These are significant differences in the economic systems of the four countries, which will help to shape the newly emerging structures of economic democracy in these countries.

When we come to economic planning, we find that the French tradition of strong central government has facilitated the development of continuing, organised arrangements for economic planning. In the USA, on the other hand, where strong central government is traditionally anathema, national economic planning has not existed. Britain comes half way between France and the United States: economic planning has not been ruled out, but it has been fitful and half-hearted. In Japan, as in France, economic planning appears to have been successful. But in Japan as compared with France, the role of government is more limited. By coordinating different interests it can help a consensus to develop. But unlike the French government it cannot exercise real leadership, except when this arises from a consensus with business leaders.

The role of the elites is another feature of the economic

system which differs from country to country. In Britain the economic elites are separate and static: people generally make a career in politics, the civil service, industry or the City, and remain in one of these. Personal links and mobility between politics, the civil service, industry and the City have been rare. In France, by contrast, there exists something more like a single elite of people who have known each other since they started their careers together in the Grandes Ecoles, and who circulate between government, industry, finance and politics. The United States comes somewhere between Britain and France in this respect. Leading people circulate readily through business, government and finance; but, partly for geographical reasons, they do not constitute a single centralised elite, based on the capital city.

Many other factors play an important part in shaping the economic system in any particular country. For example, Britain's economic system has evolved more or less uninterruptedly over the past century or so. In the United States also the economic system has evolved uninterruptedly since the Civil War, but greater modernity and wider frontiers have allowed more rapid change than in Britain. In Germany and Japan on the other hand, the destruction of industrial plant and economic institutions in the second world war meant that in many respects a new start was necessary and possible in 1945.

The way in which the economic system develops is also affected by the general climate of opinion towards the business community. In Britain influential sections of society have always been anti-business, going back to the churches, universities, armed forces, learned professions and rural gentry of the 18th and 19th centuries. In Germany on the other hand, pro-business sentiment has always been stronger, while in the United States the business of business has been the business of America. Clearly, cultural traditions of this kind will affect the manner in which economic democracy comes about. In the United States today, for example, business leadership still seems to take initiatives, whereas in Britain business leaders have been on the defensive for many years.

Finally, a brief word about ideologies. George Lodge[23] says that a synthesis of the world ideologies is taking place. He suggests that we can notice this growing synthesis if we place the ideologies of the world today on a spectrum, with the United States at one end, communitarian China at the other end, and Britain, France, Germany, the USSR and Japan ranged in between them. Lodge concludes that, if a world ideological synthesis is indeed occurring, it is important to analyse and describe this synthesis 'so that it can function fully in designing such new world institutions as transnational corporations'. I agree with this. I believe that today's ideologies are in fact beginning to converge towards a new planetary ideology of the future which will be based on sanity, humanity and ecology (SHE). I have no doubt that the converging ideologies of today, and the beckoning ideology of the future, will help to shape the new structures of economic democracy as they continue to emerge.

Future Institutional Changes

In his study of business civilisation in decline, Robert Heilbroner[15] concluded that the demise of the business system is likely to proceed by degrees, insensibly altering a civilisation that can be called 'capitalist' into one that, whatever we decide to call it, will be very different. Heilbroner envisages a tightly controlled society in which the traditional pillars of capitalism — the legitimacy of private property and the operation of the market mechanism 'have been amended beyond recognition, if not wholly superseded by state property and state directives'. In the more distant future, Heilbroner finds it possible to imagine an eventual dissolution of centralised power. But he does not think this can possibly occur for a long time to come. Heilbroner, living in capitalist America as does J. K. Galbraith, perceives as does Galbraith[39] that capitalism is being superseded, and that this means a greater involvement by the state in economic matters. What North American thinkers do not find it so easy to perceive as we who have lived through the last thirty years in countries like Britain and France, is that the practical limits to centralised state control are quite quickly reached, and that decentralisation then becomes necessary.

In the first part of Chapter 2 I quoted Peter Jay's view[27] that 'democracy has itself by the tail and is eating itself up fast'. Jay describes the political economy of the industrialised democracies as 'one in which governments can periodically be dismissed by the vote of the people and in which the labour market is free except insofar as the principal suppliers of labour voluntarily agree from time to time that the freedom shall be modified for a while. In this circumstance — and given general familiarity with the short-term potentialities of deficit finance — the maintenance in the short as well as the longer run of a very high level of employment becomes a political imperative. This can be achieved only at the cost of an accelerating rate of inflation, which must sooner or later destroy either the freedom of the labour market (with or without the consent of the main suppliers of labour) or the high level of employment. Since either or both of these consequences are outside the tolerance of the electorate, no government will be able to satisfy the electorate; and therefore the system of political economy is inherently unstable.'

Thus Jay agrees with Heilbroner that the present institutional structure of the economy in industrial countries like Britain and the United States cannot last much longer: 'the contradiction of existing political economy' can only be resolved by changing the economic mechanisms which at present face governments with a choice between politically unacceptable unemployment, politically unacceptable interference in the labour market, and an inherently unstable policy of inflation. But Jay does not accept that this change must involve the introduction of authoritarian state control. In his view it could be achieved if working people were able to come to terms with 'the entrepreneurial realities which concern their present employers, so that they will accept a non-inflationary market-determined environment as setting the level of rewards that can be afforded'. In other words, Jay recommends the re-introduction of a market economy, but a market economy in which the economic units (i.e. individual enterprises) are owned, controlled and managed by the workers. He puts this forward as an alternative to capitalism, state socialism, and to the form of corporate state which is evolving today in

Britain and other western industrial countries.

Norman Macrae, the deputy editor of the 'Economist', is another who believes, like Jay, that decentralisation rather than further centralisation of economic activity will and should take place. But Macrae's approach is different from Jay's. In a recent survey[40] on the coming entrepreneurial revolution, Macrae forecast that the age of big business corporations is probably drawing to its end; these institutions may now be at their peak; during the next two or three decades they may virtually disappear in their present form. They will not, in Macrae's view, be replaced by state capitalism; indeed, many services now provided by government will be returned to competitive private enterprise. Incentives to make workers happier will be individually designed, so as to allow everyone to choose their own lifestyles. Dynamic corporations of the future will try several alternative ways of doing things in competition within themselves. The role of their workers, as individuals or as group co-operatives, will be as entrepreneurial subcontrators. In Macrae's words, successful big corporations will have devolved themselves into confederations of entrepreneurs.

In practice, the economy of the future will probably not be wholly dominated by the state (Heilbroner and Galbraith), or by worker-managed enterprises (Jay), or by decentralised confederations of entrepreneurial groups (Macrae) — though all these three kinds of institutions may play important economic roles. But what can be said with certainty is that, if an equilibrium economy replaces an expansionist one, the characteristic economic institutions would themselves be based on the principle of balance, not aggrandisement. The first aim of business enterprises, financial institutions, and economic agencies of government, would not be to grow or expand or maximise, but to balance the interests of their main stakeholders — workers, customers, investors and the public — and thus to preserve corporate equilibrium.

The idea that this balancing of the interests of *all* the various stakeholders will provide a more genuine form of economic democracy than worker-management — and also a more effective way of bringing inflation under control — could gather increasing momentum in some countries (like Britain) in the next few years. And it is fairly obvious that economic institutions whose first concern is balance (rather than growth or maximisation) will be appropriate for the equilibrium economy of the future.

Beyond Economics, Beyond Institutions

So far, this discussion of economic democracy has concentrated mainly on the changes taking place at the level of the nation state and within the individual business enterprise. We have not yet considered current structural changes in politics and government, which reflect the pull of greater internationalisation on the one hand and the contrary pull of devolution to regional and local levels on the other. Nor, in the context of economic democracy, have we considered the prospect of a shift of emphasis away from the formal economy towards the informal economy, which we discussed in the first part of Chapter 2.

Figure 3 outlines the unifying perspective in which all these changes should be seen. It shows that two important kinds of change are taking place simultaneously. First, as shown on the left hand side of the diagram, a process is taking place which I have called 'dismantling the nation state'.[3] We are moving out of an age in which something called sovereignty existed only at the level of the nation state, and into an age in which the vital role of government — self-government, I should say — is recognised at various different levels. Second, as shown on the right hand side of the diagram, politics is converging with economics.

In this perspective, economic democracy is seen to take many forms. At one end of the spectrum it includes measures like the drawing up and administering of codes of conduct by the United Nations to govern the behaviour of multi-national companies. At the other end it involves a more equal division of economic activity and rewards, and a more equal sharing of paid and unpaid work, between men and women in the individual household. Economic democracy also applies at every intermediate point on the spectrum, in forms appropriate to each.

The future structure of economic activity will, I believe, be

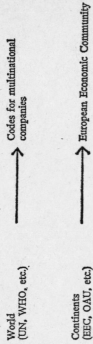
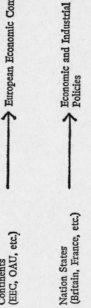

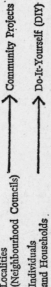

EMERGENCE OF MULTI-LEVEL GOVERNMENT

CONVERGENCE OF ECONOMICS WITH POLITICS AND SOCIETY.
Some examples:

ONLY ONE EARTH

World (UN, WHO, etc.)	→	Codes for multinational companies
Continents (EEC, OAU, etc.)	→	European Economic Community
Nation States (Britain, France, etc.)	→	Economic and Industrial Policies
Subnations and Regions (Scotland, Wales, etc.)	→	Regional Economic Planning
Cities, Counties, etc. (Local Authorities)	→	Municipalisation
Localities (Neighbourhood Councils)	→	Community Projects
Individuals and Households	→	Do-It-Yourself (DIY)

NATIONAL SOVEREIGNTY

SMALL IS BEAUTIFUL

FIGURE 3

greatly influenced by a growing awareness that economic democracy means more than changes in the institutional balance of power at the level of national economic policy, and at the level of the business enterprise. Economic democracy implies a new balance of functions and power, i.e. a new social and political balance, at every level. This new balance of functions and power will clearly be an important element in the equilibrium economy of the future; and, at the basic level of the household and local community, it will bring with it a new balance between formal and informal economic activity.

To conclude, the future structure of economic activity will thus be shaped in two main ways. It will be shaped partly by the momentum of the changes taking place today in the structure of economic institutions. Those changes are being made — in different ways in different countries according to differences in their culture and history — largely in response to political and social changes generated in the past. The resulting reforms point, at least in certain limited senses, towards greater democracy in economic affairs. But developments in the structure of economic activity will also be shaped — increasingly, I believe — not only by the push of the past, but by the pull of a new vision of the future. This will involve: a conscious and deliberate attempt to achieve an equilibrium world economy within 30 or 40 years; the rising aspiration of increasing numbers of people to become less dependent on jobs and money and goods and services of the consumer society, rather than to consume a greater quantity of material products; and a growing recognition that the institutionalised economy has reached its limits.

In these two parts of Chapter 2 I have suggested that, in the economic sphere of life, the push of the past and the pull of the future can be seen to be taking us in the same direction. Reforms in the present industrial system — initiated, contested and accepted by the existing establishment of trade union leaders, politicians, industrialists, and financiers — can be seen as steps towards the post-industrial future. In every important sphere — health, education, politics, religion, for example — a similar alignment will have to be sought between the push of the past and the pull of the future. The successful transformation of today's society into the new society of the SHE future will depend on this. The next two chapters deal with various aspects of what will be involved.

Suggested Questions for Discussion

1. Do you think that in 25 years' time economic power will be more centralised or more decentralised than today?
2. Which of the following do you think should play a more influential, and which a less influential, role in economic affairs than they do today — governments, business managements, trade unions, banks and other big financial institutions?
3. At which of the seven levels in Figure 3 do you think the idea of economic democracy is most important — global, continental, national, regional, municipal, local, household? In your own country what are the main obstacles to the further development of economic democracy?
4. Do you agree that the further development of economic democracy is likely to be one aspect of an equilibrium economy? Do you think it is likely to encourage people to become more dependent or less dependent on money and jobs?
5. Do you think of business managers as: shareholders' agents; leaders of a joint enterprise; arbiters between different interests; enablers; or something else altogether?

Suggested Reading

For the general reader

Robertson[33] Robertson[3]	focus on balance as the main structural principle of the business enterprise and the economy;
Heilbroner[15] Lodge[23] Galbraith[39]	focus on the growing role of the state in economic affairs;
Jay[27] Macrae[40]	focus on the changing structure of business enterprises.

For the more specialist reader

Prais[34] Bullock[35] Diamond[36] Drucker[38]	deal in detail with various aspects of the changing structure of modern economic institutions.

3
A Shift of Paradigms

If we are to move towards a sane, humane, ecological (SHE) future, we shall have to change the direction which modern society has been taking. In Chapter 2 we suggested what this would imply in the economic sphere, and in Chapter 2A how it could arise from present developments there. In the following chapter we shall suggest that this change of direction should be seen as a transformation.

In this chapter we discuss paradigm shifts. They will be an essential part of the required change of direction, or transformation. We describe what they are; we consider briefly how they might affect the meaning of concepts like *wealth*, *power* and *growth*; we then look a little more closely at the possibility of a shift in the prevailing paradigm of *work*, with particular attention to the way in which the transition might be made from the present paradigm to a new one; and we conclude by noting the practical need to foster and accelerate paradigm shifts of this kind.

What Is A Paradigm Shift?

A paradigm shift is the change that takes place from time to time in a basic belief or assumption (or in a constellation of basic beliefs or assumptions) underlying our perceptions and actions. It can be seen as the cultural equivalent of an evolutionary leap. A well known example is the shift, which took place in the 16th and 17th centuries and is associated with the names of Copernicus and Galileo, from the view that the sun goes round the earth to the view that the earth goes round the sun.

The concept of a paradigm shift arose from studies of the history of science. It was given currency by T. S. Kuhn in his book on 'The Structure of Scientific Revolutions'.[41] Kuhn examined 'the major turning points in scientific development associated with the names of Copernicus, Newton, Lavoisier, and Einstein. More clearly than most other episodes in the history of at least the physical sciences, these display what all scientific revolutions are about. Each of them necessitated the community's rejection of one time-honoured scientific theory in favour of another incompatible with it. Each produced a consequent shift in the problems available for scientific scrutiny and in the standards by which the profession determined what should count as an admissible problem or as a legitimate problem-solution. And each transformed the scientific imagination in ways that we shall ultimately need to describe as a transformation of the world within which scientific work was done. Such changes, together with the controversies that almost always accompany them, are the defining characteristics of scientific revolutions.'

Kuhn concluded that 'the successive transition from one paradigm to another via revolution is the actual developmental pattern of mature science. . . . When an individual or group first produces a synthesis able to attract most of the next generation's practitioners, the older schools gradually disappear. In part, their disappearance is caused by their members' conversion to the new paradigm. But there are always some men who cling to one or another of the old views, and they are simply read out of the profession which thereafter ignores their work.' The prevailing paradigm provides the agenda for all the ongoing activities of routine practitioners of science. As the paradigm shift occurs, those activities change their direction in accordance with the new paradigm.

In very much the same way as Kuhn described for science, prevailing paradigms provide the context for routine activity in non-scientific affairs, and shifts take place from one prevail-paradigm to another. For example, human beings can see themselves as outside nature, whence they can observe it, dominate it and exploit it; or, by contrast, they can feel themselves to be an integral part of nature. One aspect of the change of direction to the SHE future will be a shift from the first of these two paradigms to the second — i.e. from a scientific and economic view of nature to an ecological and spiritual view. Again, the dominant paradigm in economic affairs may be one of competition and expansion; or it may be one of co-operation and balance. A shift from the first to the second of these two paradigms will also be part of the transition to the SHE future.

In general, the paradigm shifts associated with the transition to the SHE future will reflect a shift of emphasis away from the overdeveloped, structured, exterior aspects of life towards the underdeveloped, unstructured, interior aspects — for example,

from	*to*
scientific and academic knowledge	intuitive understanding
representative politics and bureaucratic government	community politics and direct democracy
the institutional economy based on money and jobs	the gift and barter economy of households and local communities
an arm's length relationship between professionals and their clients	personally shared experience
institutionalised social services	caring personal relationships
organised religious activity and codified religious doctrines	personal spiritual experience

Key ideas in these six cases include: knowledge and learning; power and public service; wealth and work; teaching and healing; welfare and care; religious ministry and spiritual communion. In every case the prevailing paradigm can be expected to shift in much the same way: the acquisition of externally validated credentials, positions, possessions and qualifications which give one an advantage over one's less successful fellows will come to seem less important; the development of personal capacities to live one's life under one's own control, and also to help one's fellows to do the same, will come to seem more important.

One possible way of looking at these changes is to say that knowledge, power, wealth, etc. will come to be thought less desirable in themselves than we have hitherto supposed; and that thinking them desirable may become an obstacle to the good life. This corresponds to the ascetic element in much religious teaching: what the world calls good is actually bad, and for the good of our souls we should forswear it. But that is too hard for most people. An easier approach is to say that knowledge, power, wealth, etc. will continue to represent positive human aspirations; but to reinterpret what they mean.

Wealth

Here are two recent examples of rethinking about wealth. The first is a letter of mine, published in the London 'Times' on 16th February 1977.

'Lord Plowden (Letters, February 11) believes that the important thing for this country which should take precedence over everything else, is the creation of more wealth; that it is industry and commerce that create this wealth; and that from this wealth will flow new jobs, welfare and education. Most other leading people in industry, politics, trade unions, civil service and the media in Britain today still seem to share this view.

Fortunately, a great many others among us do not. We question the idea of "wealth" as something created by manufacturers of cigarettes and sweets, but not by doctors and dentists; created by bankers and commercial lawyers, but not by housewives and social workers; created by agribusiness, but not by people working their smallholdings, allotments and gardens; created by advertising agencies, but not by schools; created by the arms trade, but not by the peacepeople. Is it a law of nature that compels us to make more and more *things,* including many that are harmful or useless, before we can attend to the needs of *people?*

No, it is not. The idea of wealth as something that has to be created by the "economic" activities of industry and commerce, so that it can then be spent on something

81

quite different called "social" wellbeing, is part of the metaphysic of the industrial age. As that age draws towards its end, one of this country's greatest strengths is the great number among its people who already sense that the old metaphysic is out of date.

We, who live in the first industrial country, are now among the first to arrive at the next great turning point in history. We should take heart. In our intuitive wisdom, we are already laying the foundations for the post-industrial future, in spite of the chorus of influential voices like Lord Plowden's that urge us vainly to prolong the industrial past.'

The second is an extract from an unpublished paper called 'The New Wealth', in which Tom Burke, director of Friends of the Earth in London, suggested what wealth might mean in future.

'The new wealth might count as affluent the person who possessed the necessary equipment to make the best use of natural energy flows to heat a home or warm water — the use which accounts for the bulk of an individual's energy demand. The symbols of this kind of wealth would not be new cars, TVs or whatever, although they would be just as tangible and just as visible. They would be solar panels, insulated walls or a heat pump.

The poor would be those who remained dependent on centralised energy distribution services, vulnerable to interruption by strike, malfunction or sabotage, and even more vulnerable to rising tariffs set by inaccessible technocrats themselves the victims of market forces beyond their control. The new rich would boast not of how new their television was but of how long it was expected to last and how easy it would be to repair.

Wealth might take the form of ownership of, or at least access to, enough land to grow a proportion of one's food. This would reduce the need to earn an ever larger income in order to pay for increasingly expensive food. Wealth would consist in having access to most goods and services within easy walking or cycling distance of home thus reducing the need to spend more time earning more money to pay for more expensive transport services. A high income would be less a sign of wealth than of poverty since it would indicate dependence on the provision by someone else of a job and a workplace in order to earn the income to rent services. Wealth would consist in having more control over the decisions that affected wellbeing and in having the time to exercise that control.'

The emergence of a new paradigm of wealth as suggested by Burke will depend very largely on the practical activities of people who, in the way they live their lives, recognisably create new forms of economic and social wellbeing for themselves and others. At the same time, there is a real need for imaginative discussion and speculation about what might be meant by wealth in a sane, humane, ecological future — what would be meant by a wealthy person, a wealthy community, the creation of wealth, a rich life, poverty, and so on? How could the shift, already evident in the voluntary simplicity movement, be accelerated from today's prevailing paradigm of wealth to the new one? How did comparable shifts in the meaning of wealth occur at times like the industrial revolution, and the Renaissance and the Reformation?

Power

I have suggested[3] that the prevailing concept of power has evolved from the crudely primitive to the institutionally and metaphysically complex, and that it is now due to evolve further — towards the idea of power as the interior capacity of persons and groups of persons to control their own lives and to contribute creatively to the lives of others. In other words, the new power will be seen as the absence of dependence, and as the ability to help others to shake off dependence.

The dependence of women in a patriarchal society can be seen as a model which applies to most citizens, consumers, workers, patients, pupils and other clients of the political, managerial and professional establishment in modern industrial societies. Here is how the Boston Women's Health Book Collective[43] came to see the situation.

'Talking to each other, we realised that many of us

shared a common perception of men — that they all seemed to be able to turn themselves on and to do things for themselves. We tended to feel passive and helpless and to expect and need men to do things for us. We were trained to give our power over to men. We had reduced ourselves to objects. We remained children, helpless and giving other people power to define us and objectify us. As we talked together, we realised that one of our central fantasies was our wish to find a man who could turn us on, do for us what we could not do for ourselves, make us feel alive and affirm our existence. It was as if we were made of clay and men would mold us, shape us, and bring us to life. This was the material of our childhood dreams: "Some day my prince will come". We were always disappointed when men did not accomplish this impossible task for us. And we began to see our passive, helpless ways of handing power over to others as crippling to us. What became clear to us was that we had to change our expectations for ourselves. There was no factual reason why we could not assert and affirm our own existence to do and act for ourselves.'

These women felt they had been trained to give their power over to other people to define them. Similarly, until the Peace People came into existence in Northern Ireland, the people there had become conditioned to give their power over to the government, the political parties, the churches, the army and the paramilitaries. So we, in the rest of Britain and in other overdeveloped countries, are conditioned to give our power over to politicians and governments and bureaucracies. The concept of non-violent power, of sovereignty peacefully welling up from all the people, is relevant for us all.

The concept of non-violent power will almost certainly be central to politics in the sane, humane, ecological future. Some of the ways in which this could happen are briefly hinted in the following extract from the chairman's conclusions after a Turning Point* meeting on 'The Politics of Tomorrow', held in London in April 1977:

* See appendix.

84

'Just as the feudal church-state Europe of the Holy Roman Empire was succeeded by the nation-state Europe created by kings and the bourgeoisie, so now another Europe is emerging — a Europe of the regions in which places like Scotland, Northern Ireland and Wales will be able to develop an identity of their own.

Governments, political parties, churches, the army and the paramilitaries have all been totally unable to solve the problems of Northern Ireland. The Peace People are an exciting model for community politics, by-passing the blockages in the existing political system. As the old order breaks down, the peace movement may provide the breakthrough on which the foundations of a new society can be built.

The old order of politics and government may also be breaking down in Britain as a whole, though so far less violently than in Northern Ireland. We may need a new upsurge of non-violent community politics — the politics of the volunteer — to by-pass the blockages in the old system and break through to new patterns of political stability.'

The emergence of the new paradigm of power, as of wealth, will depend very largely on the practical activities of people who, in the way they live their lives, recognisably create new forms of power for themselves and recognisably help others to do the same. Practical training and experience in the exercise of non-violent power will play an important part. At the same time, there is a real need for imaginative and speculative discussion about what might be meant by power in a sane, humane, ecological society. Peter Cadogan's 'Direct Democracy'[44] is a good example of what is wanted here. So is 'The Price of Peace'[45] by Ciaran McKeown of the Peace People in Northern Ireland.

Growth

The concept of growth will continue, I am sure, to play a vital part in our thinking. But what kinds of growth shall we value? What kinds of growth shall we try to avoid? When, and in what circumstances, shall we prefer balance or stability to growth? As we move into the SHE future, the growth paradigm may be expected to shift from the present emphasis on tangible, impersonal, quantitative possessions and achievements to a new emphasis on less tangible, personal, qualitative capabilities and activities — from economic growth to personal and social growth.

In the economic sphere, as we discussed in Chapter 2, equilibrium will replace growth as the guiding principle. But that does not mean that growth in itself will become a dirty word. Growing will take place in other spheres. The industrial revolution has amplified our physical and intellectual capacities; our ability to care for our physical needs, to manufacture, to build, to travel, to transport, to communicate, to calculate, has grown enormously. The post-industrial revolution will amplify our psychological and social capabilities; our ability to develop ourselves, to understand one another, to support one another, to share in the life of the cosmos — that is what will grow.

Nor does the shift to equilibrium rather than growth as the guiding principle of economic life mean that all economic growth should cease. Millions of people in the world are still materially deprived; a top priority will be to enable them to meet their basic economic needs; and that will require more purposeful economic development than in the past. For most young adults there will continue to be a time when personal economic growth is appropriate. One aspect of growing up, of becoming independent from parents, is economic; and when young adults start a family of their own, their need for housing space and domestic equipment inevitably grows. When we speak of a shift of emphasis away from economic growth, it does not mean we forget these things or ignore them.

The shift to equilibrium rather than growth as the guiding principle of economic life will, however, mean a big difference in the way people think about economic growth and set about achieving it. Today, rapid growth, steady growth, low growth, no growth, negative growth, a particular percentage (e.g. 6%) growth, organic growth, differential growth, healthy growth, and good growth all have their advocates. In the SHE future we shall recognise that all these generalisations are unsound.

Economic activity is like other spheres of life: we want some things to grow, but not others. When good things grow the growth is healthy, and when bad things grow the growth is unhealthy or cancerous. Good gardening is not judged in terms of maximum, percentage or zero growth of aggregate vegetation. Good health is not judged in terms of maximum, percentage, or zero body growth aggregated over every organ and limb of a growing child. There are few important spheres of life in which reasonable people argue whether rapid, steady, low, zero, or even negative aggregate growth is the right objective to pursue for its own sake. Even statements that economic growth should be organic, differential, healthy or good will be seen to have little practical significance unless we define what specific goals and tasks they imply. And for our society to aim to increase GNP for its own sake will be regarded as just as absurd as for a person to aim at continually rising levels of money income and expenditure, regardless of what satisfaction he gets from earning an income and what satisfaction he gets from spending it.

In a chapter called 'Ideas on the Move' in his recent book,[46] Aurelio Peccei, the founder of the Club of Rome, includes a discussion of growth. He describes what is happening as follows. 'We have thus moved from gross growth to self-reliant growth and sustainable growth, and then to organic growth and dynamic equilibrium. This is tantamount to redis-covering the obvious, of which we had all lost sight in our frenzied scramble towards growth at any cost — namely that good resides in equilibrium. While these ideas are entering the common domain, another advance is being made by the recognition that there is yet another and fundamental dimension of equilibrium — within man himself. After having satisfied certain minimal requirements of life and attained physical well-being, he develops a wide range of other needs, wants and yearnings about his security, comfort, beliefs, self-fulfilment, social position, and what is generally called quality of life. Development is the word generally used to embrace the reasonable satisfaction of all such human demands, and the concept of development is rapidly superseding that of growth.' Now, Peccei continues, a further change is needed, 'a reversal of the present concept of development, bringing it to focus not on the demand side of the human being but on his capacity to contribute, hence on his quality and creativity. . . . It is wrong and misleading to consider human requirements as the starting point of a new phase of human evolution. *Development of human quality and capacity alone can be the foundation of any further achievement.* . . . This is the direction towards which we should apply all our energies if we want really "to grow".'

As the prevailing paradigm of growth continues to shift, we shall no doubt seek insights from patterns of growth in plant and animal life. For example, as the new shoots and twigs of a tree take over the process of growth from the old wood, growth ceases in the trunk and main branches. Are the over-developed industrial countries like trees in which the old wood of economic activity is hardening and reaching the limits of its growth, while the buds of psychological and social development are forming the new shoots of growth? If the tree were a rose tree or a fruit tree, we would prune it — to get new growth in the right places. Is there an equivalent way of pruning old growth in the social and human sphere? All plants and creatures have a natural life cycle — birth, growth, maturity, decline and death. Do we forget this in our attempts to prolong life, not only for individual people but also for organisations and institutions? Finally, the existence of each plant or creature to some extent enables and to some extent prevents the growth of others; and by its eventual death, it may create conditions in which others can grow. Do we tend to forget that, as individuals and as part of the institutions to which we belong, we can create conditions for others to grow in, not only by growing ourselves but also by declining? Is this what Christians mean when they say Christ died that we may live? Is it relevant to our thinking about the SHE future?

Work

The prevailing paradigm of work today conforms to the prevailing emphasis on institutionalised economic activity. The prevailing paradigm of work in the SHE future will reflect the shift of emphasis to de-institutionalised activity, and to social and psychological as opposed to economic growth. This

88

new paradigm of work, like the new paradigms of power and wealth, will see work as something which individuals and groups of people define and create for themselves, not as something which is provided for them or which they demand as the dependents of employing institutions. The shift to the new paradigm of work will be one aspect of the transformation of society, from a state in which people are encouraged to be dependent on society's institutions for all the important aspects of their lives, to a state in which people are encouraged to take control for themselves.

We start with a brief description of the present paradigm of work. We note that, as the limits close in on conventional economic growth, this paradigm is already beginning to break down. We then look briefly at what the hyper-expansionist (HE) scenario would imply for the idea of work, and we examine the possibility that work in itself will become much less important. We reject that possibility in favour of a new, but equally important, paradigm of work: which we then describe. We conclude by considering (as we did in Chapter 2A) a number of existing developments — this time in the sphere of work and employment policy — which could form a bridge between the old paradigm and the new, and which can be seen as potential steps in the transition between the industrial past and the post-industrial future.

The most important aspect of the existing paradigm is the extent to which people identify with their work. 'With the coming of the industrial revolution it was no longer enough that a man should occupy his station and give glory to God — in the world in which most of us grew up and for a number of generations prior to that time it was more essential that a man be encouraged to hold a job for which he was being paid. What are you going to be? did not refer to a child's future characteristics as a person, but to his choice of occupation.'[47] The puritan work ethic is still very much alive, in the sense that people lose status in their own eyes and in others' if they cannot get work. Moreover, the overdeveloped industrialised societies reify the concepts of work: work is a job; it is done for an employer for pay; it counts in the employment statistics. Unpaid work does not count. Unemployed people are assumed

89

to do no work. Even self-employed people suffer discrimination. National economic policies are drawn up in consultation with representatives of employers and employees, not with representatives of self-employed workers, unpaid workers and the unemployed.

As we saw in Chapter 2, however, the institutionalised economies are now reaching limits to the number of jobs, the amount of money, the quantity of goods, the standard of services, and the level of satisfaction they can provide. These limits are creating contradictions about work, which cannot be resolved within the existing paradigm.

First, work (in the form of jobs) is not available for many people who want it. This problem is continually exacerbated because, to meet the increasing demands made on the institutionalised economy for goods and services, improved productivity is always required. Whether an economy is capitalist or socialist in its structure of ownership and control makes not the slightest difference in this respect — ways are constantly being sought to produce more goods and services with less work. For employers, employing employees is a cost which has to be reduced. The result is what Keynes called technological unemployment, and he explained that it arises because 'our discovery of the means of economising the use of labour outruns the pace at which we can find new uses for labour.' This, being translated, simply means that employers — including the government as employer of last resort — tend to find ways of economising *other people's* labour faster than they can find new uses for it. It obviously is not the case that people tend to find ways of economising their own time and energies faster than they can find new uses for them. People economise their own time and energies in order to have time and energy to spend on something else. It is inherent in the institutionalisation of economic activity that it creates a demand for work in the form of jobs but provides too little of that kind of work to meet the demand.

Second, the nature of much of the work available in the form of jobs discourages people from doing it well. It is pointless and boring, if not worse, and it is alienating in the sense that it is being done for someone else — often an impersonal organisation. People no longer feel compelled to work hard at jobs which they dislike or which fail to engage their interest. The work ethic, at least in the sense of taking pride in one's work and wanting to do it well, cannot survive the increasingly widespread introduction of the kind of work which the development of an institutionalised economy involves. A new sort of work ethic may be beginning to emerge, reflecting a more discriminating attitude about how people are prepared to spend their working lives. Trade unionists are beginning to campaign not just for the traditional right to work, but for the right to work on socially useful products.[48]

Third, while the institutionalised economy fails to create enough work in the form of jobs and compels many people to do unsatisfying and pointless work in the form of jobs, much important work is not carried out at all. This includes especially the kind of work which would improve the quality of life — the creation of better surroundings and amenities, and the provision of personal care and attention to people. Work in the form of jobs is incapable of doing the work that needs to be done.

These are some of the contradictions that are closing in around the old paradigm of work, as the economies of the industrialised countries bump against their limits. It is becoming more difficult to reconcile increasing productivity with permanently high levels of employment. Because the work ethic is weakening, in the sense I have mentioned, creating new jobs in order to keep unemployment down involves paying people to be comparatively idle, and thus leads to higher public expenditure, taxation and inflation. The problem is sharpened by the rising demand from women for equal employment opportunities and equal access to unemployment benefits. And the unemployment problem is not felt by the industrialised countries alone. In 1976 the International Labour Organisation calculated that there were 30 million unemployed people in Third World countries, and that this figure was likely to rise by a further 1000 million by the end of the century.[49]

The hyper-expansionist (HE) scenario for the future claims to offer a solution to the problem of work: as super-technology and almost universal automation make more and more existing

91

work unnecessary, most people's leisure will increase; the working day, the working week, the working year, and the working life will all be reduced; most people will find their main satisfactions not in work but in leisure; the work ethic will more or less disappear. But this solution has a fatal flaw. The work ethic would not disappear for Daniel Bell's pre-eminent professional and technical class who would be responsible for the high technology and sophisticated theoretical knowledge upon which that kind of post-industrial society would depend. Their work would be of vital importance. So that kind of society would suffer from a deep schizophrenia about work. The hoi polloi would have to be persuaded that work was unimportant, unsatisfying, unfulfilling, unnecessary; while the elites and their potential recruits would have to be continually impressed with the value of work and the high status which it conferred. It just doesn't add up.

However, leaving aside the HE scenario, it is worth looking a little more closely at the possibility that the work ethic may be on the way out. Gurth Higgin discusses this possibility. As we saw in Chapter 1, his thesis[20] is that our society's traditional social project (that of overcoming scarcity) is withering; and that its leading social part (manufacturing industry) and its leading psychological part (an alienating willingness to dedicate one's life to being merely an instrument of work) are withering along with it. He expands as follows:

'Work in the service of the production of wealth is the leading part in our traditional system, and within the life space of the individual his work activity is likewise the leading part. Any approach towards improving the quality of life that is based on the assumptions of the old paradigm with economic man as its datum, whether such thinking takes the bourgeois or Marxist form, will take work as its leading part. If we are in process of developing a new social project as a more relevant paradigm, then it will be for some part of their experience other than work that people will be searching as a new leading part in their lives. No aspect of life other than work has yet become sufficiently clarified to attract the social and psychological energy of a new leading part. Nevertheless,

92

in spite of this lack of a new focus the pull of interest and energy away from the centrality of work in our lives is a fact. For many people, the idea of improving the quality of their work lives, although not unattractive, does not seem to be of central relevance to their current experience. They are more concerned to find a new and more satisfying focus for their lives than in reinforcing the declining old. In short, the quality of life is not divisible. If it considers only work, if it does not cover the total life space, for many it loses its relevance.'

Thus Higgin seems to suggest that work itself is on the way out. I do not contest that a change of the kind he discusses is taking place; but I interpret it differently. I see it as a shift of the prevailing paradigm of work, not as a rejection of work altogether. I believe that the old paradigm of work is losing credibility, and a new paradigm has begun to emerge.

My first reason for believing this is negative. What would happen if most people ceased to care about work and concentrated on leisure? What would they do with their greatly increased leisure? If their leisure activities were of the kind which costs money, increasing leisure would increase their spending. But they won't be able to earn the extra money by doing more work. So how will they get it? Who will decide how much money everyone should get to support their leisure activities? On the other hand, if their leisure is of the kind that doesn't cost money, what will people be doing with it? If they are simply wasting time, they will get bored. On the other hand, if they are entertaining one another, looking after children and sick people, doing DIY activities in the garden or house or workshop, educating themselves, writing, playing music, and a whole range of other activities which are purposeful and satisfying, as well as being enjoyable, won't they think of some of these activities as work? The more fortunate amongst us already do work of that kind today.

As David Elliott[50, 51] has pointed out, changes in our values and norms and attitudes to work and non-work could change the nature of work in the future. Today 'such activities, tasks and responsibilities as housework, child-rearing, voluntary social work and artistic creation, while being vital to the main-

93

tenance and health of society, are not perceived or rewarded as work.' But that need not always be the case. A recent Canadian report[47] suggests that the prevailing concepts of work are already changing.

'Changing concepts of work, whether at the personal or at the community or social level or both, are inescapably related to a changing sense of purpose — of what it is useful to do. . . . the labour market cannot much longer elicit credibility as an organising device for the activity of working or distributing income . . . the concept of work as something that must be socially productive in the eyes of the beholder is coming to be used to sort meaningful from empty jobs. . . . A whole new concept of work is emerging which will dismiss as work much which now passes for it and will embrace as work much which is not now included in it. . . . Local Initiative Programs and similar schemes, designed out of a labour market mentality which was concerned to "create jobs", have served another and much more important purpose, the redefining of work for some of those who were ready to move in this direction. . . . We are going to need to rely increasingly on individuals and communities to define their own concepts of work. . . . The enormous intellectual and social ferment of our times (whether we label it as future shock, or the transition to post-industrial society, the emergence of Consciousness III or the stable state, or childhood's end) is the context for changing concepts of work.'

So what can we say about the new paradigm of work which is, I suggest, already beginning to emerge?

The dominant paradigm of work in Western Europe and North America in the 19th and 20th centuries emerged from the individualist, puritan ethic which was generated by the Reformation and confirmed by the industrial revolution. As that period of history comes towards an end, will we go back to pre-industrial or pre-Reformation paradigms of work? I do not think so, at least not exactly. The traditional Roman Catholic doctrine that bodily labour was decreed by Providence for the good of man's body and soul has a too authoritarian

94

smack; it leaves the door too wide open to feudal exploitation of the work of the poor and the weak by the rich and powerful. The new work ethic may certainly have something in common with the work ethic of the Benedictine monasteries: 'Labour was to be man's greatest joy and the instrument of his union with God. Industry was the key to the upbuilding of the new world that Benedict created within the precincts of his monastic establishment. Everything was seen as an aspect of work. The singing of the divine office in church was the *opus Dei,* the work of prayer to God that is peculiar to the monk. It had to be done well. Manual labor was in its way, however, no less important in the life of the monastery, which could only exist through the support of the monk's hands. . . . Christ had redeemed human toil, making the humblest chore a labor of love. The dignity of labor was proved in the joy of a good monk's life. Work was but the highest expression of love.'[23] But even there, the notion of work as something that had to be redeemed by Christ appears to detract from the idea that work itself should be one of the main sources of human joy and satisfaction.

The new paradigm of work will, I believe, owe quite a lot to what Schumacher[24] has called Buddhist economics. He says that the Buddhist point of view takes the function of work to be threefold: to give a man a chance to utilise and develop his faculties; to enable him to overcome his ego-centredness by joining with other people in a common task; and to bring forth the goods and services needed for a becoming existence. This is not unlike William Morris's view that 'a man at work, making something which he feels will exist because he is working at it and wills it, is exercising the energies of his mind and soul as well as of his body. . . . If we work thus we will be men, and our days will be happy and eventful.'[50] But I believe that both Schumacher and William Morris under-estimated the significance of increasing economic equality between men and women, and therefore also the centrally important change that will probably take place in our relative valuation of paid and unpaid work.

I suggest that the new paradigm of work which is now emerging will see work as something which every human being should be able to take satisfaction in doing. Work, whether paid or unpaid, will signify those activities which are undertaken to satisfy human needs — one's own and other people's; and those needs will be assumed to include the higher level needs for love, esteem and personal growth as well as the basic needs for food, clothing, shelter and safety. Work will no longer be regarded as a chore — as something to be endured by the less fortunate (like the slaves in ancient Greece), to be shirked whenever possible, and ultimately to be abolished by automation. It will no longer be regarded as a job, to be created and preserved, counted and recorded, for its own sake. In a sane, humane, ecological society work will be necessary and desirable activity which confirms people in the knowledge of their own worth, which confirms the meaning of their relationships with other people, and which confirms their unity with the natural environment in which they live.

So how might the transition come about from the industrial to the post-industrial paradigm of work? What measures may be taken by today's policy-makers to deal with the problems of unemployment inherited from the past, which could turn into steps towards the new work paradigm of the future? Here are some of the questions they are having to ask.

(1) Should they accept that higher unemployment is probably inevitable, and prepare to accept the higher cost of unemployment benefits as a charge on public expenditure? The difficulty is that the present level of public expenditure, as well as the present level of unemployment, is already too high.

(2) Should they reflate the level of economic activity (by pumping money into it according to orthodox Keynesian principles of demand management) and keep it high, thereby hoping to reduce the general level of unemployment? The difficulty is that this would create more inflation, and the inflation rate is already too high.

(3) Should they go on putting large sums of public money into declining industries, bankrupt firms and other uneconomic activities including the public services, expressly in order to preserve existing jobs? As the limits

96

close in more narrowly on the number of jobs and the amount of public expenditure the institutionalised economy can generate, it might not be fair to go on giving this privileged benefit to a selected few, nor possible to give it to many.

(4) Should they continue to expand the job creation programme, especially for younger workers? Does society have an obligation to provide community service work in the first few years of some young people's working lives, while others are working as students? The net cost of increased job creation, compared with increased unemployment, is comparatively small; and it is very desirable socially that young people should have the opportunity to learn what useful work can be like. The difficulty is that increased job creation does involve increased public expenditure, and eventually there must be a limit to the amount which can be spent.

(5) In addition to creating new jobs with public funds, should they start to think how to enable people to develop new opportunities for work for themselves and others?

(6) Should they aim to bring down the retirement age and shorten the length of people's working lives? One difficulty is that, if this simply meant more people being paid more pensions for longer, it would mean heavy extra public expenditure. Another is that, unless existing attitudes to jobs and work were to change, people would bitterly resent being thrown on the scrapheap before their useful working life was finished. It would have to be recognised that people who don't have jobs, including retired people, do a great deal of socially useful and personally satisfying work in households and local communities; and that these people have a right to be provided with moral and material support by other members of their family and their neighbourhood.

(7) Should the policy-makers encourage work-sharing? Should they aim to reduce the working week to four days or possibly three? Married couples might be encouraged to share one week's work between them — but not in such a way that men go out to work all week and women stay

at home! The difficulty is that corresponding reductions in pay would be necessary in order to avoid inflation, and the trade unions would be likely to reject them. However, as more and more people come to see that occupation at home can be more rewarding economically and more satisfying psychologically than work at many existing jobs, that policy may change.

(8) Should policy-makers try to remove the stigma that still attaches to unemployment? Much valuable work is done outside formal employment, e.g. by unemployed people giving their time to community projects and other social work, by people at leisure 'doing it yourself', by houswives doing housework, or by retired people or people with private means doing charitable work. Should the policy-makers begin to play down the importance of the market economy in which people work for money and play up the importance of the gift economy in which people work for love? Should they encourage people to achieve a sense of status and self-respect by contributing to society and by serving and caring for the people with whom they deal, rather than by earning money from socially valueless or harmful work? Should they encourage a shift from an earning ethic based on the industrial paradigms of wealth and growth and work, to a new ethic of self-actualisation and caring based on post-industrial paradigms?

(9) Should policy-makers encourage people to think of occupation, not of employment and jobs? Useful occupation would comprise a spectrum of activities, including work provided by the labour market, jobs created by government, part-time paid work, temporary paid work, unpaid work carried out by people receiving unemployment and social security benefits, unpaid work by other people, special kinds of unpaid work like housework, and work done as a leisure activity. If people's prevailing concept of work were to broaden in this way, the traumatic aspects of unemployment (shortage of jobs) would be reduced.

(10) What view should the policy-makers take about economic equality between the sexes? Will it lead women to com-

pete more energetically with men for work and for pay across the whole range of a widening labour market? Will it mean that higher levels of unemployment for women than for men will be less readily accepted than in the past, thus adding both to the demand for jobs and to the total cost of unemployment benefits? Will there be increasing pressure to recognise the value of, and to pay more highly for, the kind of work that women have traditionally done — including housework? Will increasing sex equality thus create new pressures for public policy-makers in the sphere of employment and the economy, resulting in heavy new calls on public expenditure? Or, on the other hand, may increasing recognition of sex equality help to blur the traditionally sharp distinction between paid work outside the home and unpaid work in the home and local community? May this raise doubts about the monetary value of many kinds of work traditionally done by men in factories, offices and other places of work, compared with the real value of housework and other work done at home? Will men as well as women thus be encouraged to question the intrinsic value of paid as opposed to unpaid work? As a result, will more men decide they want to spend more time in the home, rather than away at a job? In this way, could increasing sex equality help to damp, rather than to increase, existing inflationary pressures for higher monetary reward and higher monetary spending? Should the policy-makers therefore encourage a shift towards a more symmetrical pattern of family life, in which husband and wife would each have part-time jobs and each take an equal share of responsibility for the home and family? Would this make it easier to adopt a three day working week? Would it encourage more people to work in, or from, or around their home and local community, on the kind of paid or unpaid work which not only has direct value and relevance for their own lives and the lives of their families and neighbours, but does not add to inflation, unemployment or public expenditure?

A few enlightened policy-makers in countries like Britain,

Canada and the United States are now beginning to explore possibilities like these, as the problem of unemployment becomes less and less amenable to solution within the framework of conventional economic policy and the industrial paradigm of work. Approaches like these not only offer a way out of the problems and contradictions generated by the industrial past; they also point towards the new post-industrial paradigm of work that is beginning to emerge.

The Task of Metaphysical Reconstruction

Our concern in this chapter has been with those ideas, or paradigms, which shape our outlook and our way of life and are embodied in our institutions. We have discussed shifts in the prevailing paradigms of wealth, power, growth and work. As we move into the SHE future, comparable paradigm shifts will occur in spheres such as health, learning, welfare and justice. These need to be worked out.

Changes in ideas and changes in activity are related to one another as chickens are to eggs. Both come first; both come second. The transformation of society results in the transformation of its dominant ideas. For example, as the prevailing forms of political and economic activity change, the prevailing paradigms of power and wealth adapt. But, equally important, the transformation of dominant ideas results in the transformation of society. As thinkers and philosophers pursue their proper task of metaphysical reconstruction (Schumacher's phrase[24]) — as they work to bring into focus a coherent constellation of new ideas about wealth, power, growth, work, etc. — the prevailing outlook and the prevailing forms of activity in society will adapt to this new framework of perception. Thus the push of events changes our thinking, and the pull of our new thinking changes the course of events.

Among the strongest reasons for doubting whether mankind will avoid catastrophe in the next 30 or 40 years is the power of vested interests and what Colin Hutchinson[52] has called the interlocked inertia of institutions. For myself, 20 years' experience of big government, big business and big finance has convinced me that people in positions of so-called power within that system have comparatively little power of constructive

100

action. Which of them can stop unemployment, or inflation, or the arms race? They are prisoners of a blocked system, trapped in an interacting complex of escalating pressures and confrontations of the kind which Gregory Bateson[53] has called schismogenic. The institutional imperative restricts the choice of acceptable solutions to those that will make the problems worse.

However, as Keynes said, 'the power of vested interests is vastly exaggerated, compared with the gradual encroachment of ideas.' The encroachment of ideas that we have been discussing here will eventually loosen the blockages in the existing institutional system. It must be purposefully pursued. The practical need is for more awareness — including more thinking, discussion and writing — about the emergence of these new paradigms and their role in society's transformation. In a sane, humane, ecological society what will most people understand by knowledge, learning, justice, teaching, welfare, caring, health, healing, growth, work, power, public service, and so on? What will be the practical consequences, as these concepts lose their present meanings and take on new ones? In aggregate, what new prevailing ideology or metaphysic will eventually be created for a new society by these conceptual changes? In the next few years these questions should be the subject of a growing spate of books, pamphlets, tracts, lectures, seminars, conferences and group discussions.

Suggested Questions for Discussion
1. How do you feel about wealth and power? Do you want more of them? Do you think your ideas about them might change?
2. How do you feel about economic growth? Is it good, bad, or indifferent? Has your thinking changed in recent years? Could the idea of personal and social growth become as powerful an energising force in the near future, as the idea of economic growth has been in the recent past?
3. Do you think growth or equilibrium will be more important as a key idea for the future?
4. Which do you think will be more important for most

people in 25 years' time, satisfaction in their work or enjoyment of their leisure? Or will the distinction between work and leisure have largely disappeared?

5. How would you start tackling the problem of unemployment? in the industrialised countries? and in the Third World?

6. How do you think increasing equality between men and women will affect our attitudes to work?

7. What changes in the prevailing ideas of health, education, justice, and welfare would correspond to the changes in wealth, power, growth and work discussed in this chapter?

8. How would these changing ideas about wealth, power, growth, work, etc. affect your present working life as a business manager, trade unionist, banker, government official, lawyer, accountant, doctor, teacher, housewife, or whatever your job actually is?

Suggested Reading

Robertson[3]: new concepts of power and wealth.
Schumacher[24]: new concepts of work and wealth.
Kuhn[41]: scientific revolutions and paradigm shifts.
Cadogan[44] } power, non-violence, personal
McKeown[45] } and community politics.
Peccei[46]: new concepts of growth; world development.
Elliot[50]: changing concepts of work.
Hutchinson[52]: changing lifestyles.

4
A Process of Transformation

Moving into the SHE future will involve a change of direction
in the development of modern societies — a transformation of
society and of ourselves. This process will be immensely complex. It will be accomplished more smoothly if we understand
its nature. So in this chapter we consider what kind of a
direction change this will be, and we discuss various aspects of
the transformation process. We thus prepare the ground for the
discussion of practical action in the final chapter.

Upward Spiral

What kind of a direction change should we envisage, then,
as we turn towards the SHE future? I suggest that we think of
the five competing scenarios in the following way.

A Business-As-Usual future would imply that we continue to
proceed in the same general direction as hitherto, and a little
upwards; unspectacular progress would continue. The Disaster
scenario would imply that we plummet downwards, losing much
of the ground we have gained in the past. The TC future would
imply that we freeze things and stay where we are without
much hope of upward progress, in order to secure the ground
we have gained already. The HE future would imply a deliberate
acceleration of dominant recent trends, in a marked upward
and forward movement. The SHE scenario can best be understood as an upward spiral, in the sense that we shall move
upward to better things while also, in certain respects, doub-
ling back on the past. For example, we shall put great emphasis
on self-help as was done by Samuel Smiles and others in the
19th century; but we shall not leave people to go to the wall
if they fail; we shall enable them to help themselves. Again,
more work will come back into the home and the local community; but on a democratic basis, without returning to
patriarchal domination in the home or squirearchical domination in the local community. Yet again, more of us will live

more self-sufficient lives on our own piece of land than in modern industrial society; but advanced small-scale technology will enable us to live much better than our pre-industrial ancestors did. The idea of an upward spiral has many applications of this kind.

Breakdown/Breakthrough

The coming transformation can also be understood as a process of breakdown and breakthrough — breakdown of the old and breakthrough to the new.

Powerful trends are combining to create a breakdown in existing values, existing lifestyles and existing institutions. These trends include: domination by big technology, exhaustion of natural resources, pollution, unemployment, inflation, a general paralysis of institutions, widespread personal helplessness, and so on. Meanwhile, new growth points are emerging which could converge to create a breakthrough to a new and better society. These new growth points include: a new emphasis on self-help, self-reliance and self-sufficiency; a new balance between the sexes; a growing interest in social, economic and political structures which serve people rather than dominate them; a growing commitment to appropriate technologies which do the same; a growing feeling that we are all inhabitants of the same planet, citizens of the same world; a growing ecological consciousness; and an increasing interest in a spiritual and cosmic approach to life, summarily described by the terms supernature and supermind.

Another way of looking at breakdown/breakthrough is closely relevant to the paradigm shifts discussed in Chapter 3. Overdeveloped institutional and intellectual structures can be seen as an important part of what is beginning to break down, and personal experience and action an important part of what should be encouraged to break through — as follows:

breakdown	breakthrough
scientific and academic knowledge	intuitive understanding
representative politics and bureaucratic government	community politics and direct democracy

the institutional economy based on money and jobs	the gift and barter economy of households and local communities
an arm's length relationship between professionals and their clients	personally shared experience
institutionalised social services	caring personal relationships
organised religious activity and codified religious doctrines	personal spiritual experience

The relationship between the first and second of each of these opposing pairs — as also the relationship between city and country, between industrialised and Third World peoples, between men and women, and between the left and right sides of the brain — has become very asymmetrical in the modern industrialised world, to the point where the first has overshadowed and threatened to suppress the second. As the well-known religious thinker Raimundo Panikkar has put it in a somewhat different context, 'Applying *logos* to the myth, amounts to killing the myth: it is like looking for darkness with a torch.'[54] Applying laboratory tests to spiritual healing, or bureaucratic scrutiny to community self-help, or cost-benefit analysis to social innovation, destroys the conditions in which spiritual healing, community self-help or social innovation can take place — like looking for darkness with a torch. But now these asymmetrical relationships are beginning to break down. In every case the same kind of questions are beginning to arise — about creativity and the upsurge of new aspirations. In every case a new relationship will have to be developed. It will be based on harmony and balance rather than on domination and subservience. It will be achieved by decolonising the old structures and liberating the new energies.

These concepts of decolonisation and liberation are crucial. If an old order is breaking down and we want a new one to break through, two principal tasks clearly present themselves. The first is to manage the breakdown of the old order in such a way as to avoid catastrophic collapse and untold hardship for the vast majority of people who depend upon it for almost every aspect of their lives. The second is to foster the growth points which will eventually provide the foundations on which a new society can be built. The first is a task of decolonisation; the second is a task of liberation. They are, of course, the two sides of a single coin.

Many recent thinkers about the transformation — or revolution — which we now face, concentrate on the second of these two sides only. Murray Bookchin's essays[18] on 'post-scarcity anarchism', 'ecology and revolutionary thought', 'liberatory technology' and 'forms of freedom' are good examples of the best thinking of the 1960s and early 1970s. They emphasise the centrality of liberation: 'The problems of social reconstruction have been reduced to practical tasks that can be solved spontaneously by self-liberatory acts of society. . . . A libertarian society can be achieved only by a libertarian revolution. Freedom cannot be delivered as an end-product of a revolution.' Now, of course it is perfectly true that people cannot be given power, they must take it for themselves and create it by their own learning in action — just as adolescents must do their own growing up. But at the same time it is a great mistake to forget the other side of the picture. Those who have power can learn to give it away before it crumbles — they can help other people to take it, just as enlightened parents can help their adolescent children to grow up.

Decolonisation

People who continue to work in the institutionalised and professionalised structures of society — as politicians, civil servants, businessmen, industrialists, bankers, scientists, teachers, doctors, planners, trade unionists, and so on — have a vital part to play in the coming transformation of society. But they must decide which side they are on. Are they working for some variant of a hyper-expansionist, elitist, institutionalised, authoritarian future — the TC or HE futures of Chapter 1 — in which people like themselves will dominate other people? Are they simply coasting along in their comparatively privileged position? Or are they ready to commit themselves to work for a sane, humane, ecological future? Do they recognise that, as Ivan Illich has said about scientific discoveries, their expertise can be used in two different ways, and are they prepared to choose the second? 'The first leads to specialisation of functions, institutionalisation of values and centralisation of power, and turns people into accessories of bureaucracies or machines; the second enlarges the range of each person's competence, control and initiative, limited only by other individuals' claims to an equal range of power and freedom.'[55] Are they prepared to use their skills, their experience and their position to enlarge the range of other people's autonomy? Are they prepared to give away their own relative superiority?

There are already signs of professional people trying to develop an enabling role rather than a dominating one. Some remarks made at a recent conference in Ottawa on the future of the serving professions[56] will serve to illustrate the possibility of professionals helping their patients, customers and clients to become less dependent on them and to increase their self-reliance.

> 'The institutionalisation of service-providing bureaucracies turns the client into a consumer, creating yet another barrier between the professional and the real person.'

> 'Professionals should share rather than monopolise their privileged knowledge, give people a chance to learn while they are healing.'

> 'Until a conscious majority brings about economic and social changes to provide the basis for a truly human society, a sane society, we all can only do our best, wherever we are, to demystify, expose, act *with* people on problems, not *for* them.'

> 'The individual has little feeling for participation in our present society because of social structures in which the professions hold a major power base. Is radical social change possible, given the present state of professional institutions?'

> 'The professions are as subject to the "greatest crisis of our times", the personal identity crisis, as anyone else

in contemporary urban society. Without their professional definition many would feel extremely threatened. Is it realistic, given the alienating nature of our cities, to expect people to give up these identities?'

'Professionals as a group have abdicated their responsibility in terms of effecting social change.'

'Are professionals prepared to give up middle class standards and prestige in order to get closer to those they serve?'

'Lawyers under the present system are paid antagonists hired to fight with one another on behalf of others who want expertise with non-involvement.'

'If poverty is basically the absence of power, social action must involve giving people part of this power back. We lawyers should be training people to understand the law and apply it to represent themselves.'

'This "Me God, you stupid" attitude of the doctor towards the patient, which stems from professional insecurity, is a kind of refined violence.'

'The question we must seriously ask ourselves is to what extent are we as physicians prepared to disappear? What we should be asking in our relationships with patients is "What have I done so this person can manage to do without me in the future?" '

'Among the social pitfalls fostered by the professions is the trend towards overdependency which verges on helplessness. Among the questions we professionals must ask ourselves is whether we are helpers or hinderers. Are we creating an endless production of services that draw us further into a trap? Do we, through the framing of laws and other structures create barriers that we then must spend valuable time breaking down again?'

Here are a few other examples of the idea that managers and professional people should help people to help themselves, rather than monopolise their expertise so as to keep people dependent on them. The Association of Karen Horney Psychoanalytic Counsellors[57] has been set up to aid untrained people to gain skills in psychoanalytic self-analysis. It aims to build up a basic group of highly skilled counsellors and teachers, and to introduce co-operative methods on as wide a scale as possible. It intends also to train people working in neighbourhood, community, voluntary and health projects. In a completely different field, the Royal Bank of Canada has recently begun to set up Community Branches, designed to provide banking services 'to people on welfare as well as to the working poor, in order to begin to build bridges from the culture of poverty into the mainstream of Canadian life. This includes counselling and referral services and provides meeting space in front of the branch for the people in the community so that they can teach themselves how to manage their funds, assess their financial problems, and derive workable solutions.'[58] John Turner and his colleagues in the architectural and planning professions are developing practical concepts of 'freedom to build' and 'housing by people', as opposed to the conventional assumption of most housing, building and planning agencies, and most of their professional and administrative agents, that any new or newly perceived housing problem must be perceived as a demand for a new programme.[59] Alice Coleman[60] has argued for an approach to environmental planning which will enlarge people's options rather than restrict them; for example, environments can be designed in which a large range of destinations — homes, shops, workplaces, schools, hospitals, and so on — are located within short distances of one another, thus giving people genuine options of walking or cycling.

This enabling ethic is applicable to every sphere of organised life, including business, government, trade unions, the public services, communications and the media, and entertainment. It would provide the underlying principle for the decolonisation of institutionalised society. It suggests that people who work in government, business, trade unions and finance, should act so as to reduce people's economic dependence on jobs, on money, and on goods and services provided by industry, commerce and the public services. It suggests that people who are trained and experienced journalists, broadcasters, managers and technicians in the press and broadcasting media, should help their existing and potential readers, listeners and viewers to become less dependent on them for their information and entertainment. In Chapter 5 we shall suggest a comprehensive basis for discussing the practical possibilities. But here are some examples for business and government.

Oil companies have seen their role in industrial society as selling increasing quantities of oil. In the SHE society, oil companies will aim to help their customers to buy less oil, by reducing their dependence on it. In other words, the nature of the oil business will change from producing and selling oil, to helping people to be more self-reliant in meeting their energy needs. Similarly, pharmaceutical and food manufacturing firms have set out to sell increasing quantities of drugs and convenience foods. In the SHE society they will help their customers to reduce their dependence on these products. The nature of the business will then have changed from producing and selling health products and food products, to helping people to meet their health needs and food needs in a more self-reliant way.

So far as governments are concerned, instead of continuing to build up capital-intensive industry, centralised energy systems, and bureaucratic public services, thereby increasing people's dependence upon them for work, for material needs and for social wellbeing — governments will shift the emphasis to policies which help people to become more self-sufficient and autonomous. For example:

> they will support *decentralised* energy production and conservation;
> they will develop *job creation programmes*, not so much as a centralised policy for providing more jobs, but in order to foster economic self-reliance at the local community level;
> they will encourage the kind of *investment in housing and other local facilities* (including gardens, workshops, etc.) which would help to develop the economic and social self-reliance of households and local communities;
> they will encourage *rural resettlement* and small-scale agriculture.

Those then are the kinds of changes decolonisation will involve. Now for some of the problems.

110

For a start, there is the problem of domination and dependence. For many of the people in managerial, professional and governing positions, their personal identity and their lifetime's energy are invested in the importance of their present role and in the sense of other people's dependence on it. They will feel threatened by the possible loss of their existing position and their existing power, and they will cling to them neurotically. John Adams has said of the logical and mathematical models of society which so many social scientists try to use: 'Such models . . . many represent for some shrunken souls the essence of society. But rather I suspect they represent a retreat from a reality that is too alarming to contemplate. They represent a proper Laingian case of schizophrenia, in which a real world that is frightening and obviously out of control is replaced by a more comforting fantasy world in which the planner is master.'[61] As the old system continues to break down, many managers, professionals, politicians, trade union leaders and other established leaders are likely to make increasingly authoritarian attempts to bolster the importance of the knowledge and skill, experience and power, which they have built up within it. At the same time, there will be many citizens, consumers, workers, patients and other clients of the existing structures who will cling to their dependence. They will feel threatened by the thought of having to take power and responsibility to themselves.

Some managerial and professional people will also have a genuinely altruistic reluctance to abdicate from responsibility. Many people believe that the decolonising imperial powers abdicated their responsibilities in the 1950s and 1960s. Certainly there are places, such as Uganda, where decolonisation has been followed by a reversion to disorder, violence and tyranny. Many responsible people will genuinely fear that to decolonise the present institutions of industrialised society would be to abandon millions of people — who now depend on those institutions for physical, material and psychological security — to the tyranny of local rulers, the exploitation of local tycoons, the domination of local patriarchs, and the magic of local charlatans and witch doctors.

At the practical administrative level, routine practitioners

111

will find it hard to justify 'enabling' policies according to the conventional criteria used by governments, business managements and the professions today. For example, suppose that a government decided to invest public money in a housing programme which would provide sufficient garden and workshop facilities to enable the occupants to become less dependent on money for buying food and household items, and less dependent on the labour market for work. Not only would the direct financial return on the investment be 'uneconomic' (according to conventional criteria about rates of return), but the investment would actually reduce the level of measured GNP. So, although a housing policy of this kind might be very successful and valuable in social and human terms, it would be unthinkable according to conventional criteria. No doubt there will be many examples in spheres such as education and health, where enabling policies will be impossible to justify by the conventional criteria used to evaluate new proposals today.

These difficulties and problems will be very real. They will not be solved theoretically in advance, but by the cumulative weight of new developments which show that in practice they can be overcome or ignored, and which thus erode their relevance. Abraham Maslow throws light on this aspect of transformation, on the process of transition from an old paradigm to a new one, when he speaks of tolerating 'the simultaneous existence and perception of inconsistencies, of oppositions, and of flat contradictions. These seem to be products of partial cognition, and fade away with cognition of the whole.'[62] Many people already recognise that the conventional criteria of profit and economic surplus are products of partial cognition.

Decolonisation was a historic task, a high endeavour, for many colonial administrators earlier this century. This was expressed as follows by the senior British official in one African territory writing confidentially to his colleagues in 1951 at a time of local crisis. 'One thing which is quite certain is that we are following the policy which is the British contribution to world political history. . . . We need to recapture our mission, and to remember what we came to this country to do: to work for the wellbeing and the progress of the people . . .

112

not to seek too much for ourselves, but to be the instruments of carrying out our country's policy loyally and tirelessly. And that policy is to lead these people onwards to govern themselves, and eventually to decide for themselves what their future status as a country is to be. . . . We have instilled democratic ideals into them; we have taught them to wish to govern themselves; the growth in political consciousness and in critical attitudes to the actions of government is what our own education and our own outlook on life and affairs have given them.'[63] The best among the British colonial administrators always knew that they were working towards the achievement of their own redundancy. The roots of this policy went back many years to the Durham Report on Canada in 1837. Its culmination was marked by Mr. Harold Macmillan's 'wind of change' tour of Africa as Prime Minister in 1960. As we face the prospect of decolonising the overdeveloped institutions of industrialised society, we shall no doubt have something to learn from the successes and failures of Britain's and other European countries' colonial policies in the 19th and 20th centuries.

Liberation

If managing the breakdown of overdeveloped institutions can be seen as decolonisation, developing one's own and other people's self-reliance can be seen as liberation. In health, in education, at work, in housing, in food, in transport, in energy, in politics, in religion, and in other economic and social aspects of our lives, many of us need to liberate ourselves and others from excessive dependence — on money and jobs; on big organisations, big technology, and professionalised services; on cities; on men, if we are women; on the industrialised countries if we live in the Third World; and on logic and the intellect, if our intuitions and emotions have been stunted and underdeveloped.

We can imagine this liberation movement as a post-industrial revolution, which parallels the industrial revolution in various important features. The industrial revolution, of course, was about technical and economic innovation and development, whereas the post-industrial revolution will be

113

about psychological and social innovation and development. That is the distinction to keep in mind, as we consider possible parallels with the industrial revolution that began in 18th century Britain — relying heavily for this purpose on Peter Mathias' 'The First Industrial Nation'.[68]

The first significant point is that the industrial revolution by-passed the established order. There was no question of conscious government policy sponsoring industrial progress. The industrial revolution occurred spontaneously, behind the back of the state and of the ruling classes of the time. We may expect the post-industrial revolution similarly to by-pass the established order today. If the dominant institutions of industrial society — government, industry, finance, trade unions, public services, universities and professions — are uninterested in promoting psychological and social innovation and growth, that is no cause for alarm.

Second, government in 18th century Britain was more permissive towards new economic activity than in other countries like France. Moreover, the social structure and social attitudes of 18th century Britain were more flexible than in any other European country, except perhaps for Holland. Increasing religious heterodoxy meant that various groups, particularly of Protestant non-conformists like Quakers, were developing their own social ethics and economic roles along with their own theology. Today, prevailing attitudes of permissiveness and flexibility towards social and psychological innovation are likely to provide fruitful conditions for the post-industrial revolution; and among today's (not religious, but secular) non-conforming groups we are likely to find its active pioneers.

Third, one of the main pre-requisites for the industrial revolution was the existence of economic resources sufficient in quantity and conveniently positioned to develop new dimensions to the economy. In 18th century Britain plentiful coal and iron ore were conveniently placed for water transport in many parts of the country, and a strategic river system, based on the rivers Trent and Severn, stretched into the heart of industrial England. A corresponding pre-requisite for the post-industrial revolution will clearly be the existence of social resources sufficient in strength and so related to one another that from them

114

can be developed new dimensions to society. These social resources could include: large numbers of active people leisured or unemployed; large numbers of active people educated and socially aware; the existence of education, information and communication systems which are not altogether closed to new ideas, not altogether dominated by economic, social and political forces committed to the status quo; and a widespread awareness that psychological and social development has become as important, if not more important, than economic and commercial development.

Another factor in the industrial revolution was inventiveness, a readiness to use other people's ideas and skills, and the capacity to generate an increasing flow of technical innovations through which physical production and productivity could be increased. The post-industrial revolution will also need inventiveness — to generate an increasing flow of social innovations, through which the psychological and social counterparts to physical production and productivity can be increased. These will be to do with teaching, learning and the sharing of new consciousness.

Again, a new breed of entrepreneurs played a special part in the energetic experimentation and technical innovation which marked the industrial revolution. These were the men, Mathias says, 'under whose charge new sectors of the economy could be developed and inventions brought into productive use. Such men were the shock troops of economic change.' In the post-industrial revolution entrepreneurs of social change will play a comparable role, facilitating new types of social and psychological growth and helping to bring social and psychological innovations into widespread use.

Innovation in industry in 18th century Britain also required the investment of financial capital in the productive process. New channels had to be created, through which savings could flow to the people who wanted to use them from the people who had spare money to invest. In due course there developed a linked national network of financial institutions, including the country banks, and the bankers, billbrokers and other specialist intermediaries in the City of London, to handle the transfer of credit from one part of the country to another; and the habit of productive financial investment became established. What will be the post-industrial counterparts to financial capital, to the banking networks, and to the habit of productive financial investment? Instead of money, shall we be concerned with psychological and social energy? Will there be people with surplus psychological and social energy to invest in other people's projects, in the confident expectation of receiving psychological and social — rather than commercial — reward from their investment? What sort of people are these, what is the nature of their support for the social entrepreneur, what reward do they seek, how shall we identify them, and how shall we create the channels to link them with the social entrepreneurs and social innovators who need their backing? Will networks like the Scientific and Medical Network* or Turning Point* provide such channels? Will activist minorities, linked with one another and receiving support through these and similar networks, provide the shock troops for the psychological and social changes of the post-industrial revolution?

To sum up, the industrial revolution was a self-sustaining cumulative process of industrial innovation centred upon what Mathias calls the 'new matrix of industries, materials and skills', in which steam power, coal, iron machinery, and engineering skills played the dominant part. This new matrix gave increasing freedom from the limitations of the physical capabilities of human beings which had held back economic activity in all previous ages. We should expect the post-industrial revolution similarly to become a self-sustaining process, in which a new matrix of psycho-social resources, techniques and skills (corresponding to Mathias' matrix of industries, materials and engineering skills) will give increasing freedom from the limitations of personal and institutional capabilities which have held back psychological and social growth hitherto.

Imagining the new liberation movement in this way, participating in its specific activities, and understanding and communicating its progress as it develops, will all be important ways of helping it to come about. Realism will be needed. Many new endeavours will fail, though they may make a

---

* See appendix.

positive contribution nonetheless. People will only support a new initiative if it offers something they want and seems likely to be a better use of their time and energy than other ways of spending them. Although the main objective of these endeavours will not be technological achievement or financial profit, they will fail if they are technically incompetent or financially irresponsible. Many charlatans, tricksters, cranks, free riders and born losers will join this bandwagon, as they have done with every other new movement in history, and it will often be difficult to distinguish them from genuine pioneers. Effective partners in this new social revolution will need good judgement and staying power as well as enthusiasm and new age values.

The Psychology of Transformation

The idea of a breakdown of an old way of life and a break-through to a new one suggests parallels with the decline of the old and the growth of the new in nature's cycles: death and birth; evening and morning; winter and spring. It may also remind us of situations in our personal lives, when the end of one phase and the beginning of another is accompanied by regret for what is over, grief for past failure, hope for the future, expectation of things to come. Some people see in it a parallel with religious ideas of death and resurrection, and think of the 'evolutionary leap into the new age made by the Son of Man'.[65]

It is possible to view the present crisis of mankind as a crisis of adolescence, a time of change from dependence and irresponsibility to independence and responsibility. The SHE future requires the internalisation of social control (for example in worker managed or socially responsible business enterprises) and the development of personal and group self-reliance. The SHE future can thus be seen to depend on society's development from childhood to adulthood, whereas the regulations and controls of the TC future would imply that childhood continues. The relationship between decolonisers and liberators can be understood as a relationship between parents and growing up children.

On the other hand, Stephen Verney[65] argues that the challenge before us is to grow from independence to interdependence. He says, 'It is commonly suggested that mankind is now coming of age, which is taken to mean, by those who use the phrase, that we are arriving at mature wisdom. But a boy or girl comes of age at eighteen, and this is not the time of mature wisdom but the end of adolescence. It is the stage when he or she is emerging from a rebellion against parental authority and preparing for marriage, and for making a responsible contribution to society. If the Renaissance can be understood as a period when we in Europe broke out of a hierarchical order into an age of individualism — if at least the emphasis of that collective change was from dependence to independence — then we might understand our own generation as a time when the emphasis must be on interdependence — we must stop behaving like irresponsible adolescent individualists.'

Or perhaps we are going through a mid-life crisis. Gurth Higgin[66] describes this as a centroversion crisis, and explains as follows: 'The individual dominated by an active thrusting ego goes through the first half of life establishing a job and a family and settling an adult identity. . . . He has little trouble from his internal world. This is damped down and contained. . . . But then comes what is usually called the mid-life crisis. . . . It is precipitated by a lessening of ego activity. . . . The individual comes to realise that his life, job or career pattern is settled. . . . The ego slows down a little, softens its outward thrust. The whole system relaxes and reflects. . . . All the wondering questions about identity, about the value for himself of what he does with his life, about what he believes in, plague his mind. . . . There is only finite time — is he doing what he really wants to do, is he really the person he really wants to be?' Peter Draper,[29] a doctor, takes a similar view in his advice to the British economy: 'You seem to be going through a kind of middle-age crisis, you are on the edge of a new phase of life, what some social physicians have called a "post-industrial" state. Try to sort out what it is you want to accomplish; talk about it, so that appropriate courses of action will make themselves more apparent. And don't please, go on holiday with any of the other hypochondriacs in your neighbourhood. If you need company, choose friends who can concentrate on goals and values. You have the age and experience to sort things out — and only you can decide what you want to make of your life.'

Willis Harman[4] has drawn attention to the fact that breakdown/breakthrough is a component in the transformation both of individuals and of societies. He says, 'All we have learned of psychotherapy suggests that it is at the precise time when the individual feels as if his whole life is crashing down around him that he is most likely to achieve an inner reorganisation constituting a quantum leap in his growth towards maturity. Our hope, our belief, is that it is precisely when society's future seems so beleaguered — when its problems seem almost staggering in complexity, when so many individuals seem alienated, and so many values seem to have deteriorated — that it is most likely to achieve a metamorphosis in society's growth toward maturity, toward more truly enhancing and fulfilling the human spirit than ever before. Thus we envision the possibility of an evolutionary leap to a trans-industrial society that not only has know how, but also has a deep inner knowledge of what is worth doing.'

The coming transformation of society will be accomplished more effectively and peacefully if we understand the practical psychology of it. For example, it is not hard to guess that dominant and dependent character types will resist decolonisation and liberation, since their sense of security rests on domination or dependence; and it is fairly obvious that most people whose livelihood, welfare and identity depend on business or finance, politics or government, the public services or the trade unions will feel threatened by the new paradigms of wealth, power, growth and work discussed in Chapter 3. What is not yet clear — at least to me — is precisely how the insights of psychology and psychotherapy should be used to help us to overcome these resistances and insecurities. How, for example, could the principles and techniques of transactional analysis[67] be used to encourage the replacement of the existing pattern of domination/dependence (Parent/ Child) relationships in society by a new pattern of interdependent (Adult/Adult) relationships? How can our growing understanding of the connections between character type and

119

work roles (for example, in business corporations where the interactions between such types as 'jungle fighters', 'company men', 'craftsmen' and 'gamesmen' have been extensively studied[68]) be applied to the interactive dynamics of a transformation process involving society as a whole? Psychologists and sociologists might be able to help us here.

A Multitude of Roles

The sane, humane, ecological society will be a pluralist, polymorphous society. Its members will not aim to develop a uniform approach to life, based on a single dominant perspective or point of view — such, for example, as is implied by utilitarianism, cost/benefit analysis or attempts to improve existing methods of 'measurement of economic welfare' (MEW). It will be a society in which learning to share the perspectives of other people, other cultures, other religions, is recognised as an important aspect of personal and social growth. It will be a society which reflects the dynamic equilibrium of ecological systems in nature.

The transition to the SHE future will also be a pluralist, polymorphous process. It will reflect the processes of biological evolution, as understood by contemporary scientists: 'Evolution, it now appears, is not an orderly progression in which one type replaces another, but a complex flux of shifting dynamic equilibriums.'[69] Many different types of people, interacting with one another in different roles, will help to transform our existing society. Different countries will also play different parts. We need to accept the reality of this. No one's particular perspective on events or the particular field in which they are capable of making their own contribution, will be *the* one which matters. No one will be in a position to draw up a master-plan for the transition. The very idea of a master-plan for the SHE future is a contradiction in itself.

Among the people whose interactions with one another in the coming years will positively shape the process of transforming our present society into a sane, humane, ecological one, will be the following:

(1) people whose aim and skill is to speed the breakdown of the old system, by helping to make it inoperable and

120

destroying its credibility; theirs is a *demolition* role;

(2) people who oppose proposals for change which would lead society in a hyper-expansionist or authoritarian direction; these include, for example, opponents of the spread of nuclear energy; theirs is an *opposition* role;

(3) people who are trying to improve the old system, by introducing changes which will make it better and stronger; their aim is to avert the breakdown of the old, but their actions may help to ease the transition to the new; theirs is a *reforming* role;

(4) people who are creating and developing the growth points for a new society; theirs is a *construction* role;

(5) people who aim to liberate themselves and other people from their present dependence on the existing system of society; theirs is a *liberating* role;

(6) people who are working to ensure that the old system breaks down as painlessly as possible for everyone who is dependent on it ;they are managing its collapse; theirs is a *decolonising* role;

(7) people who, as liberators or as decolonisers, are helping other people to take more control over their own lives — in health, or politics, or learning, or religion, or their economic activities, or in any other important aspect of their life; theirs is an *enabling* role;

(8) people who are changing their personal way of life, and helping other people to change theirs, so that their lives will be more consistent with their image of a sane, humane, ecological future; theirs is a *lifestyle* role;

(9) people who are exploring and communicating new concepts of power, wealth, work, growth, learning, healing, and so on, appropriate to a sane, humane, ecological society; they are the paradigm shifters, the ideological revolutionaries; theirs is a *metaphysical reconstruction* role;

(10) and, finally, people who recognise that all these different sorts of people will contribute positively to the transformation of society, and who are working to make sure that the transformation, though polycentric, is a widely understood, widely shared process of conscious evolutionary change; theirs is a *strategic* role.

We should not forget other people too, whose contribution to the transformation will be negative or neutral. They include:

(11) people who refuse to countenance the breakdown of the old system and its replacement by a new one; they will try to suppress the activities of the people listed in the previous paragraph; theirs is a *reactionary* role;

(12) people who, having themselves failed in their own attempts to change society in one way or another are confident that no one else will succeed, and anxious that they should not; they include Nestorian wiseacres, but mainly theirs is the *pessimistic and cynical* role;

(13) people who are humble (or superior) observers of what is happening; they enjoy talking about it, writing about it and scoring points off one another about it, but they don't want to take part; they can be helpful or unhelpful; theirs is the *academic* role;

(14) and, finally, people who just want to get on with their own lives in whatever circumstances happen to exist; they are not particularly concerned to encourage change or to resist it; theirs is the *routine practitioners'* role.

How will all these different sorts of people interact, as the transformation gathers pace? We cannot tell in detail in advance, but we should try to be prepared.

Different countries, as well as different individuals and groups will also have their own parts to play in the coming transformation of society.

It may have been true, as Murray Bookchin says, that every revolutionary epoch in the past has focussed upon a specific

122

country where the social crisis was most acute — England in the 17th century, France in the 18th and the 19th, and Russia in the early 20th century. Moreover, there may still be an understandable tendency to think that one's own country is especially well placed to play a leading part in the impending transformation. Bookchin,[18] for example, argues that 'the center of the social crisis in the late twentieth century is the United States — an industrial colossus that produces more than half of the world's goods with little more than five percent of the world's population. Here is the Rome of world capitalism, the keystone of its imperial arch, the workshop and marketplace of its commodities, the den of its financial wizardry, the temple of its culture, and the armory of its weapons. Here, too, is the center of the world counter-revolution — and the center of the social revolution that can overthrow hierarchical society as a world-historical system. . . . America, it must be emphasised, occupies the most advanced social terrain in the world. America, more than any other country, is pregnant with the most important social crisis in history. Every issue that bears on the abolition of hierarchical society and on the construction of utopia is more apparent here than elsewhere. Here lie the resources to annul and transcend what Marx called the "prehistory" of humanity. Here, too, are the contradictions that produce the most advanced form of revolutionary struggle.'

There are those of us, from Britain, on the other hand, who have claimed that the first industrial nation, the country of Adam Smith and Karl Marx, is now the first to reach the limits of industrialism; it is Britain, we think, that is now pioneering — reluctantly and only half-consciously perhaps — the post-industrial revolution. In this connection I was struck by a real paradox when I travelled in the United States and Canada in 1976. There seems to be a much greater ferment of intellectual interest there than in Britain about what the future will be like — about the possibility that modern societies may develop in radically different directions from the recent past. Reputed business thinkers at places like Stanford and Harvard are teaching and writing on such topics as the changing American ideology, voluntary simplicity, and new images of man. In

Ottawa, the Vanier Institute for the Family is questioning the present view of society, and working towards an alternative perspective in which individuals, families and local communities will take pride of place. This seemed a far cry from the kinds of things that happen in most business schools and Royal Institutes in Britain. There is also more practical experimentation in the United States (especially, but not only, in California) with new ways of living and new forms of consciousness. The paradox is that, even if the so-called opinion formers in Britain seem much less interested, our whole society is, in fact, already struggling with the future, trying to cope in practice — if not in theory — with what happens when industrial societies come to the end of the road. In spite of all the intellectual ferment, the USA has not yet reached that stage of practical involvement: there is still much more space there — wider physical boundaries, more economic room for manoeuvre, more psychological space — if you don't like where you are in your life or your work, there is still somewhere else to go.

However, I suspect the truth is that constructive optimists in every country feel that theirs is specially well placed to take part in the evolutionary breakthrough to a new future. After all, each country, like each individual, has its own unique perspective, its very own set of problems and opportunities, hang-ups and insights. Learning to understand how other countries are likely to experience the change of direction towards the polymorphous SHE future, will itself be part of the change.

Suggested Questions for Discussion
1. Imagining the future as an upward spiral, how many ways can you think of in which the future might be like the past, but at a higher level?
2. Assuming that an old order is breaking down and a new one is beginning to break through, what would you personally see as the most important things that are breaking down and the most important things that are beginning to break through?

124

3. Are you personally more concerned about the transformation of society as a whole, or about changes in yourself and other people close to you? What common ground do you find between people whose main concern differs in this respect?

4. Which is better for people: either to be dependent on, and perhaps exploited by, bureaucratic organisations and professional experts; or to try to be more self-reliant, without so much protection from charlatans and bully-boys?

5. Can you think of ways in which people might break out of existing psychological and organisational limits to personal growth, much as the industrial revolution enabled people to break out of previous limits to economic growth? What actual or possible social inventions and innovations can you think of, which would compare with important technological inventions and innovations?

6. Do you think your country's present problems are more like a crisis of adolescence or a mid-life crisis?

7. Which of the fourteen different roles mentioned in the last section of this chapter corresponds most closely to your own present role? Which of the fourteen do you most admire? Which do you most dislike?

8. Which countries do you think are well placed to play a leading part in the post-industrial revolution?

Suggested Reading

Verney[65]
Harman[4]
Jungk[70]
} three complementary approaches — religious, humanistic, multifarious — to the coming transformation of society.

Bateson[53]
Higgin[6]
} psychological, anthropological, and sociological aspects of the transformation process.

Illich [71 72 72 73]
Turner[59]
} aspects of decolonisation.

Bookchin[18]
} aspects of liberation.

5
Pieces of the Action

Previous chapters have discussed what the impending transformation of society might be like. This chapter, which is short and practical in intention, is concerned with action to help to bring the transformation about. After some general points about this kind of action, a method is proposed, with which readers are invited to experiment, for identifying *transformation activities*. A project is then described in which readers are invited to participate for a clearinghouse of information and ideas. Finally, the chapter contains a list of people and organisations, which may be useful as an illustration of some of the things that are happening already, and perhaps also as a source of contacts and further information.

Most of the people who actively help to bring about the transformation to the SHE future will not be doing so from a sense of duty, or because other people have told them they ought. Nor will they be obeying orders or regulations from above. They will be doing so because that is how they want to spend their lives. Living more frugally in a material sense in order to live more richly in a personal sense, concentrating on personal and social growth rather than economic growth, enabling other people to become more self-reliant — these will be the kind of things they find fulfilling for themselves. As in the industrial revolution, or in the great surge westward across America in the 19th century, the main breakthroughs will be made by energetic people carving out the new frontier, occupying new space for themselves, and blazing a trail for other people to follow. The main initiatives will not come from moralisers preaching, nor from policy-makers and bureaucrats imposing a grand plan for change.

Thus the pieces of the action will be very numerous. The people and organisations listed in the appendix, and the writers and publications in the list of references, cover a very wide range of activities and subjects. They include: disarmament;

126

conservation; Third World development; alternatives in agriculture, education, health, energy, technology, economics, and housing; community politics and neighbourhood self-reliance; decentralisation; campaigns for sex equality; new consciousness techniques; and many others. The transformation of society will be achieved by a multitude of people like these doing their own things.

There will often be room for argument whether particular activities (or people, or organisations) are part of the problem or part of the solution; do they hinder or help the transition to the SHE future? For instance, if you fly by jet-plane all over the world to tell people that they should use bicycles instead of energy-expensive transport, is your message likely to be more effective than your example, or vice versa? If you take up self-sufficient organic farming, after making a lot of money as a stockbroker, which of those two ways of life will you be an advertisement for? If you make local common ownership in industry an issue in national politics, will you be helping to decentralise economic activity or will you simply be confirming the business-as-usual processes of centralised power? Because people who are trying to live for the future have to live in the present, questions like those can be asked of almost everybody. It is probably best to ask them critically about your own activities and sympathetically about other people's, and then trust your judgement in both cases.

Egotism and cliquishness are part of the human condition. Activists for change sometimes seem especially vulnerable to them. By being too possessive about their activities, they often underestimate what other people are doing and repel their co-operation. The same thing happens on a larger scale when people identify themselves with a banner or a label or a leader. When we become members of a political party, or a professional organisation, or a trade union, or followers of Christ or Marx or some other leader or guru, we become opponents to people who are marching in the same direction under another banner. Much of our energy and theirs is then siphoned off into secondary activities directed to the maintenance of our particular club or clique and to the propagation of its proprietary doctrines. Many people cannot manage without clubs and cliques and banners and labels and leaders and doctrines of this kind, but it is very important to try to minimise their debilitating effects.

Activists should also stop to consider whether their activities may seem threatening to other people. Alvin Toffler has made us all familiar with the concept of future shock;[74] the prospect of the future — even thinking about the future — can be frightening for many people. So if you want people to take an interest in your hopes for the future, you may have to take the trouble to calm their fears. More positively, it is sometimes tempting to try to put the fear of God into lazy, privileged, complacent, short-sighted members of the existing establishment. This may serve a useful purpose, in certain circumstances. But usually not. It should always be a matter for deliberate decision whether frightening people is likely to be helpful, unhelpful or immaterial to what you are trying to do.

A Framework For Thought and Action

The following suggestions are offered as a practical device for stimulating productive thought and action, and for facilitating communication. I would ask that readers experiment with them and then perhaps try to improve them, before seeking reasons to reject them out of hand. As a general rule, too much discussion about the future — especially by academics — consists of negative attempts to dispute or discredit what other people propose.

I have taken six important *transformation roles* (from among the roles enumerated in Chapter 4), and I have combined them with thirty important *activity areas*. The combination gives 180 different *transformation activities*.

The six transformation roles and thirty activity areas are listed below. An example of a transformation role is *Lifestyles*; this means changing your way of life to be more consistent with your vision of the SHE future. An example of an activity area is *Work and Employment;* this means the kind of work you do and the way you do it. Combining the Lifestyle transformation role and the Work and Employment activity area gives the following transformation activity: changing your way of life so that your work is more consistent with your vision of the SHE future.

In practice, real-life activities cannot be neatly parcelled up into 180 or any other number of different compartments. But, as I hope to show, this basic framework does — if sensibly used — provide a valuable stimulus to new thinking and action, and a good basis for comunication about different activities on different parts of the new frontier.

The six transformation roles are as follows:
A. *Lifestyles*: changing one's personal way of life so that it is more consistent with the SHE future.
B. *Enabling (Liberation)*: fostering new growth points (e.g. alternative technology, common ownership in industry, Yoga techniques) which help people to liberate themselves from dependence, to become more self-reliant, and to develop their autonomy.
C. *Enabling (Decolonisation)*: managing the breakdown of existing institutions, relationships, etc., so as to help previously dependent people to become more self-reliant, and to develop their autonomy.
D. *Metaphysical Reconstruction*: creating new visions of the SHE future, developing new paradigms, and communicating them.
E. *Strategy*: mapping the transition to the SHE future; identifying pitfalls and unresolved problems; and providing opportunities for communication, information exchange, and cross-fertilisation.
F. *Opposition*: opposing and attempting to obstruct activities — such as the construction of fast-breeder nuclear reactors, or practices perpetuating racial or sex discrimination — which tend in the direction of the Business-As-Usual, Disaster, TC, or HE scenarios.

The thirty activity areas are as follows:
1. Families, Households and Local Communities
2. Roles of the Sexes
3. Roles of Children, Adults and the Elderly
4. Land Use and Land Tenure
5. Agriculture and Food

6. Conservation of Minerals and Materials
7. Manufacture, Repair and Maintenance of Things
8. Provision of Services and Care to People
9. Politics and Government
10. Economic Organisation
11. Management
12. Energy
13. Transport
14. Cities, Towns and Rural Resettlement
15. Housing
16. Roles of Professions
17. Science and Technology
18. Health
19. Education
20. Money and Finance
21. Work and Employment
22. Religion
23. Arts and Culture
24. Leisure, Entertainment and Sport
25. Information and Communications Media
26. Crime, Prisons, Police, Law, etc.
27. Defence and the Military
28. Third World
29. European Community
30. Disarmament and Peace

In order to imagine the use of this conceptual framework to stimulate ideas and action, let us take some combinations at random.

A1 — Lifestyles & Families, Households and Local Communities — means changing one's way of life so as to play a more balanced part in the life of one's family, household and local community. It might, for example, include changing from a full-time to a part-time job; or changing from full-time housework to a part-time local job.

F30 — Opposition & Disarmament and Peace — means acting in opposition to military expansion, weapons development, the arms trade, etc., in the cause of disarmament and peace. It would apply to people in the peace movement, and to pressure group activities of an anti-military character.

B10 — Enabling (Liberation) & Economic Organisation — means acting to encourage the development (by liberation) of new forms of economic organisation which exist to serve people. It would include the activity of a group of employees who are striving to turn their enterprise into a common ownership or worker co-operative.

C10 — Enabling (Decolonisation) & Economic Organisation — means acting to encourage the development (by decolonisation) of new forms of economic organisation which exist to serve people. It would apply to the directors and managers of a large business enterprise who hived off a subsidiary part of it and enabled it to operate independently as a common ownership or worker co-operative.

D15 — Metaphysical Reconstruction & Housing — means creating and disseminating new ideas about housing, appropriate to the SHE future, as John Turner has recently done in his book 'Housing by People'.[59]

B26 — Enabling (Liberation) & Crime, Prisons, Police, Law, etc. — means acting to encourage decentralisation and greater personal autonomy in the field of crime, prisons, etc. Two widely different examples would be: a campaign to encourage private individuals to conveyance their own house purchases; and the activities of the Delancey Street Foundation in San Francisco, which helps criminals, drug addicts and drop-outs to rehabilitate themselves.[75]

E1 — Strategy & Families, Households and Local Communities — means helping to develop a strategy for strengthening the role in society of families, households and local communities. The work of the Vanier Institute of the Family (see appendix) is an example.

D19 — Metaphysical Reconstruction & Education — means creating and disseminating new ideas about education, for example as Peter Abbs and Graham Carey have done in 'Proposals for a New College.'[76]

D22 — Metaphysical Reconstruction & Religion — means creating and disseminating new ideas about religion and cosmology, for example as Henryk Skolimowski has done in his recent Tract on 'Ecological Humanism'.[78]

Using the Framework

Any of the 180 transformation activities would provide a useful subject for a brainstorming discussion to identify as many possible ways of carrying out that activity as the participants could suggest. For instance, a discussion about energy might focus on possible examples of C12 — Enabling (Decolonisation) & Energy. Participants would be encouraged to think of all the initiatives that could be taken by governments, nationalised industries, oil companies, other businesses and industries, scientists, trade unions, etc., to enable energy users to become more self-reliant in meeting the energy needs of their households and local communities. Or in a discussion of E14 — Strategy & Cities, Towns and Rural Resettlement — people would be encouraged to think of as many ways as possible of mapping the transition from today's over-urbanised situation (with 2% of working people in agriculture in a country like Britain) to a situation in 30 or 40 years' time in which 10% might be working in agriculture.

These 180 transformation activities can also be used as a basis for organising information. Through the Turning Point network and in other ways I receive information and requests for information about people and organisations who are working for the SHE future. The next stage in the development of this clearinghouse operation will be to organise it according to the framework I have just described. I would be glad if readers would send me, or ask me for, specific information or specific suggestions about activities in one or more of the 180 categories A1 to F30. Most real-life activities will overlap several categories. That does not matter.

This kind of clearinghouse operation will provide a sketch-map of the new territory being opened up by a multitude of scattered pioneers and settlers. It will help people to work out where they are in relation to one another, what they have in common, where they could go next, who is there already, and who might be able to help them on their way. In return, the experience of pioneers and settlers will help to improve the map. This is itself an example of the kind of shared strategic thinking that is needed for the transition to the SHE future.

Summary

Most of the people who are actively and usefully involved in the transition to the SHE future will be doing their own thing in one or another (or several) of a multitude of different ways. Although this book has touched on only a few, I hope it has conveyed an impression of how wide ranging they are.

Important pieces of the action (belonging to the E—Strategy —transformation role) revolve round the need to encourage productive discussion and thought which lead to further action. This book is one item which is intended to stimulate such discussion and thought, and I hope it will be useful to many different kinds of people.

Special arrangements are needed to bring together tripartite discussion groups of *activists, professionals,* and *laypeople* (as was mentioned in the Introduction). I would be glad to hear from readers interested in taking part.

A clearinghouse for information, broadly organised according to the transformation roles and activity areas outlined in this Chapter, will be one among the growing number of network centres which are active in the field of alternative futures. I am involved in developing a clearinghouse operation on these lines. If readers have information or requests for information about transformation activities, I would be glad to receive them.

Suggestions For Discussion

1. Think of your own work, position in society, way of life, etc. Identify combinations of transformation roles and activity areas (as described in this chapter) that could be directly relevant to your situation. Discuss what practical changes they might suggest in your life.

2. Think of other types of people and their work, positions in society, etc. — e.g. a politician, a banker, a teacher, a doctor, a trade union leader, a scientist, etc., etc. Identify combinations of transformation roles and activity areas that could be directly relevant to each of them. Discuss what practical changes they might suggest for those people's work and lives.
3. Discuss how changes like these in the work and lives of some people could affect other people's lives, and thus how they could contribute to changing society as a whole.
4. Think of constructive ideas, or relevant facts, or practical requests for advice or information, that you would like to send to the author of this book, after reading it and discussing it.

People and Organisations

This list of people and organisations illustrates the wide range of activities relevant to the SHE future. With a few exceptions those listed are known to me personally. Many of the people have spoken at Turning Point meetings. My apologies in advance to any who would prefer not to have been included, or who would have preferred me to describe them differently.

Many other people and organisations might have been listed. For example, all the main political parties in Britain now have their environmental or ecology association, and there is a new Ecology Party. There is a wide range of alternative publications, such as the Ecologist, Undercurrents, Peace News, Resurgence. There are one or two people in most of the business schools and management centres who are concerned about the future and sympathetic to some of the ideas in this book. The same might be said of government departments, big companies, consulting firms, universities, and professional associations. And there are many other individuals who might have been included if I had more space.

Most of those listed are active centres of practical information and ideas. In general, they will probably be glad to hear from people whose interest is constructive and helpful. Many of them offer a newsletter (or membership) to which one can subscribe. But they are mostly busy people, often without the resources or time to deal with unproductive enquiries. If you get in touch with them to ask for information or advice, consider whether there is any help or support you might be able to give them in return.

Britain

PETER ABBS, Gryphon Press, 38 Prince Edwards Road, Lewes, Sussex. Editor of "Tract", a non-profit journal critical of industrial civilisation, for people who wish to have a general grasp of current thinking about education, culture, ecology and sociology. Also co-author of "Proposal for a New College".[76] Alternatives in education.

JOHN ADAMS, Geography Dept., University College, London WC1. New approaches to transport and planning. Published criticisms of obsolete economics, conventional methods of traffic forecasting, cost benefit analysis, systems analysis, etc.

ALTERNATIVE SOCIETY (Foundation for Alternatives), The Rookery, Adderbury, Nr. Banbury, Oxfordshire (Stan Windass). Now concentrating on housing, health, employment and rural resettlement. Lower Shaw Farm, Swindon (Dick Kitto) now operates independently as a residential centre for meetings connected with alternatives.

PATRICK ARMSTRONG, One World Trust, 24 Palace Chambers, Bridge Street, London SW1. Parliamentary Group for World Government. Also "Learning for Change in World Society".[80]

MARGARET BARNETT, Church Broughton, Derbyshire. Soil Association, Farm and Food Society, McCarrison Society, Henry Doubleday Research Association. Conservation, food, organic farming.

DAVID BERRY, 45 Bromley Common, Bromley, Kent. Futures research and communications. London branch of the World Futures Society.

DR. FRED H. BLUM, New ERA Centre, Flaunden, Hemel Hempstead, Herts. Concerned with the development of people as creative and responsible participants in the process of transforming consciousness and the social order.

C. MAXWELL CADE, Audio Ltd., 26-28 Wendell Road, London W12 9RT. Courses in self-control and self-development based on the modern science of biofeedback and the ancient traditions of yoga and meditation.

PETER CADOGAN, 1 Hampstead Hill Gardens, London NW3. Humanism, direct democracy, non-violence, peace, South Place Ethical Society. Author of "Direct Democracy".[44] Co-founder of Turning Point.

DR. PETER CHAPMAN, Energy Research Group, Physics Dept., Open University, Walton Hall, Milton Keynes MK7 6AT. Options, strategies, choices for energy policy. Author of "Fuel's Paradise."[77]

JOHN COLEMAN, The Nook, Hook Village, Warsash, Southampton. Common Market Monitoring Association. Parliamentary Liaison

Group for small businesses and the self-employed. Decentralisation.

CONSERVATION SOCIETY, 12A Guildford Street, Chertsey, Surrey KT16 8BR. (Dr. John Davoll) Population, resources and the environment. Membership, branches, working parties, "Conservation News", conferences, etc.

PROFESSOR S. L. COOK, University of Aston Management Centre, Maple House, 158 Corporation Street, Birmingham B4 6TE. Interdisciplinary research and social progress. Operational research in the service of society.

MIKE COOLEY, 95 Sussex Place, Slough, Bucks. Campaign for the right to work on socially useful products, originated by the Lucas Aerospace Shopstewards Combine Committee.

RENEE-MARIE CROOSE PARRY, Flat 7, 81 Onslow Square, London SW7. The future, new values, peace, disarmament, "People for a Non-Nuclear World", founder of the Teilhard Centre for the Future of Man.

GUY DAUNCEY, Holne Cross Cottage, Ashburton, Devon. Writer. Sherrack (local community magazine in Devon). Unemployment and work. Alternative futures. Evolution of consciousness.

JOHN DAVIS, c/o Intermediate Technology Development Group, Parnell House, Wilton Road, London SW1. Appropriate technology for the UK. Newsletter (six-monthly) from 10 Grenfell Road, Beaconsfield, Bucks.

DR. ANTHONY DEAVIN, 101 Dora Road, Wimbledon Park, London SW19. Organic farming. Better use of land. Bridge Trust (establishes centres for co-operative, organic farming; crafts and skills; retreat, quiet and healing).

PAUL DERRICK, 30 Wandsworth Bridge Road, London SW6. International Co-operative Alliance. Robert Owen Association. Christian Socialism. Co-operation and common ownership in industry.

PETER DRAPER, Unit for the Study of Health Policy, Dept. of Community Medicine, Guy's Hospital Medical School, 8 Newcomen Street, London SE1 1YR. Economic policy and health, community medicine, effects of the mass media, humanism.

DAVID ELLIOTT, Faculty of Technology, Open University, Walton Hall, Milton Keynes, MK7 6AT. Alternative technology, the future of work, "Undercurrents". Author.[50, 51]

ENERGY 2000, 64 Salisbury Road, Sheffield S10 1WB. (Richard Turner — Organiser.) Opposes nuclear power, encourages alternative scenarios of energy consumption and production. Supported by MPs from the main political parties, and by the National Union of Mineworkers.

NICHOLAS FALK, 12-13 Henrietta Street, Covent Garden, London WC2. Economic regeneration of inner cities. Rotherhithe workshops. URBED (Urban and Economic Development) newsletter about small enterprises in city centres. Conferences and seminars. Also active Fabian.

ALEC AND NORAH FORBES, 5 Thorn Park, Plymouth, Devon PLG 4TG. Healing Research Trust. Encourages alternative therapies — acupuncture, healing, naturopathy, radionics, etc. Information and advice, newsletter, local groups, etc.

FRIENDS OF THE EARTH, 9 Poland Street, London W1V 3DG. (Tom Burke). Conservation, restoration and rational use of the ecosphere. Campaigns on energy, recycling, wildlife, transport, food, etc. Local groups, supporters' bulletin.

FUTURES NETWORK, c/o J. M. Williamson, Inter-Bank Research Organisation, Moor House, London Wall, London EC2Y 5ET. An informal association of people — mainly from the business, government, trade union and management sectors — to exchange information and views about futures research and the use of futures thinking.

FUTURES STUDIES CENTRE, 15 Kelso Road, Leeds, LS2 9PR. (Roland Chaplain). Useful newsletter, diary of events, etc. Conferences on Industry, the Community and Appropriate Technology.

PROFESSOR GURTH HIGGIN, Dept. of Management Studies, University of Technology, Loughborough, Leicestershire LE11 3TU. Continuing Management Education. Participative self-management. "Barefoot" models of organisations and professional activities. Author of "Symptoms of Tomorrow".[66]

RONALD HIGGINS, Little Reeve, Vowchurch Common, Hereford HR2 0RL. Author of "The Seventh Enemy".[8]

TONY HODGSON, 1 Castle Mill House, Juxon Street, Oxford OX2 6DR. Strategic management. Design of participative "workshops". Miniaturisation of agriculture. Research for the Institute for the Comparative Study of History, Philosophy and the Sciences.

HOUSING EXCHANGE NETWORK. Contacts: *International*, John F. C. Turner, Development and Planning Unit, Bartlett School of Architecture and Planning, University College, London; *National*, Peter Stead, Associated Housing Advisory Services (AHAS), 3 Provost Road, London NW3; *London*, Bertha Turner, 30 Greenwood Road, Hackney, London E8. Encouragement, help, advice and co-operation to achieve greater personal and local autonomy in housing — "housing by people".

KEITH HUDSON, 79 Sutton Avenue, Eastern Green, Coventry CV5 7ER. Employment, conservation, economics, etc. Formerly editor and publisher of "Towards Survival". Currently co-ordinator of Jobs for Coventry, a project under the job creation programme.

COLIN HUTCHINSON, Kingswood, Beatrice Road, Oxted, Surrey. Independent consultant on the management of change. Past chairman of the Conservation Society. Author of "Crisis of Lifestyles".[52] Co-founder of Turning Point.

BRIAN JOHNSON, IIED, 27 Mortimer St., London W1. Environment, third world development, questions of political and economic scale, international organisations. International Institute of Environment and Development. Recent publication: "Whose Power To Choose: International Institutions and the Control of Nuclear Energy".

FRANCIS KINSMAN, 28 Vardens Road, London SW11. Economic, financial and political forecasting. Inventor of the TAROT (Trend Analysis and Relative Opinion Testing) method of forecasting.

UNA M. KROLL, 46 Rosehill Avenue, Sutton, Surrey SM1 3HG. The role of women in the church. The Christian Parity Group.

KRISHAN KUMAR, Keynes College, University of Kent, Canterbury, Kent CT2 7NP. Co-ordinates research for the Acton Society. Interested in the possibility that Britain, having been the first industrial society, may also be the first post-industrial society.

RONNIE LESSEM, City University, Graduate Business Centre, Lionel Denny House, 23 Goswell Road, London EC1M 7BB. Management education for a changing society. Courses in alternative forms of management.

THE LUCIS TRUST, 235 Finchley Road, London NW3 6LC. (Mrs. Winifred Brewin). The activities of the Lucis Trust are based on the writings of Alice Bailey. They see the present as a time of preparation for a new civilisation and culture, a new world order, and a new spiritual dispensation.

COLIN MARSH, Dept. of Civil Engineering, University of Newcastle-upon-Tyne, Claremont Road, Newcastle-upon-Tyne NE1 7RU. Appropriate technology. Conferences and scientific papers.

PATRICIA ELTON MAYO, Penbryn Hall, Montgomery, Powys, Wales. Decentralisation in politics. A future Europe of the regions. The ethnic groups of Europe. Author of "Roots of Identity".

MARCUS AND MARIKA McCAUSLAND, Health for the New Age, 1a Addison Crescent, London W14 8JP. Positive health education, community health care, integration of conventional and unconventional therapies into a form of health care which deals with the whole person.

BILL AND SANDRA (MASON) MARTIN, Lint Growis, Foxearth, Sudbury, Suffolk. Independent leisure consultants. The future of work and leisure. Two scenarios for leisure in the 1980s.

NATIONAL CENTRE FOR ALTERNATIVE TECHNOLOGY, Llwyngwern Quarry, Pantperthog, Machynlleth, Powys, Wales. (Roderick James). A permanent exhibition of alternative technologies (windmills, solar panels, solar heated house, etc.), and horticulture. Newsletter, bookstall.

NEW MILLS, Luxborough, Watchet, Somerset TA23 0LF. (Rhys Taylor and Michael Brown). A rural alternative project. Publishes a useful newsletter of contacts in England's Environmental Movement.

PEACE PEOPLE, 8 Upper Crescent, Belfast 7, Northern Ireland. (Mairead Corrigan, Betty Williams, Ciaran McKeown). The Northern Ireland Peace People are well known for their public stand against violence in Northern Ireland. They are also a non-violent community movement, with community projects and a community newspaper, "Peace By Peace".

MICHAEL RIDDELL, Ockenden Venture, Guildford Road, Woking, Surrey. Communications. Wide range of contacts among "New Age" thinkers: Findhorn, Festival of Hope, Festival of Mind and Body, etc.

PATRICK AND SHIRLEY RIVERS, Field Gate, Brockweir, Chepstow NP6 7NN. Self-sufficient smallholding. Patrick also writes — e.g. "Living Better on Less."[81]

SCIENTIFIC AND MEDICAL NETWORK, Lake House, Ockley, Near Dorking, Surrey RH5 5NS. (George Blaker). A network of scientists, medical people and philosophers with a common interest in a spiritual and non-materialistic world outlook. They promote paraphysical and parapsychological studies, and organise courses and conferences.

SCOTT BADER, Ltd., Wollaston, Wellingborough, Northamptonshire. (Godric Bader, David Ralley). Pioneering common ownership enterprise, which aims to give "the best possible service to our fellow men", and to "the general welfare of society, internationally, nationally and in the company's immediate neighbourhood".

SENSE (Skills Exchange Network for a Stable Economy) 18 The Forum, Chidham Park, Havant, Hants. Publishes a news-sheet about courses, events and people concerned with bee-keeping, glass-blowing, goat-farming, plumbing, weaving and many other skills.

GEOFF SMITH, Bracken Cottage, Chilver House Lane, Bawsey, King's Lynn, Norfolk. Independent management consultant, specialising in the use of added value as a basis for business success, employee participation, etc.

KEN SMITH, Staple Farmhouse, Staple, Canterbury, Kent. Food/small scale technology co-operatives. Skill Centre for Canterbury Unemployed Youth. Scientific and Medical Network. Alternative science/technology youth projects. Deschooling.

SOUTH LONDON INDUSTRIAL MISSION, 27 Blackfriars Road, London SE1 8NY. (Rev. Canon Peter B. Challen). Practical involvement in the industrial problems of the modern city. Job creation and unemployment. New approaches to wealth, work, growth, etc.

VAL STEVENS, 77 School Road, Hall Green, Birmingham B28 8JQ. Green Ban Action Committee, Friends of the Earth, Conservation Society, Population Countdown. Environmentalism and the trade unions.

MANUELA SYKES, 8 Sussex Street, London SW1. Job creation. Encouragement of worker co-operatives and common ownership enterprises in a London borough. Also: Industrial Common Ownership Movement (ICOM), 31 Hare Street, Woolwich, London SE18.

THE TEILHARD CENTRE FOR THE FUTURE OF MAN, 81 Cromwell Road, London SW7 5BW. Conferences, seminars, journal, newsletter. Evolution of consciousness. Mankind's responsibility for the future. The Teilhardian approach recognises the value of all human experience, faith and culture and does not seek the dominance of any one system.

HARFORD THOMAS, 82 Hillway, London N6. Freelance journalist. "Guardian" columnist. Alternatives. Quality of life. Third world. Small businesses. "Places for People". Sovereignty welling up from the people.

TURNING POINT, 7 St. Ann's Villas, London W11 4RU. (Alison Pritchard). A network of people mainly in Britain, North America and Europe, who share the view that mankind is at a turning point. Wide range of concerns — environment, sex equality, third world, disarmament, community politics, direct democracy, and alternatives in education, economics, health, agriculture, religion, etc. Conferences, seminars, newsletter.

BOB WALLER, 175 Earlham Road, Norwich NR2 34G. Writer (author of "Be Human Or Die"), humanist, environmentalist, campaigner. Land and agriculture. Conservation Society, Council for the Preservation of Rural England, Open Spaces Society, Street Roots Group, Alliance against Norwich Airport.

North America

PROFESSOR RUSS BEATON, Willamette University, Salem, Oregon, USA. Alternative Futures Project, developing techniques of experimenting with alternative futures as one aspect of education.

ANNE W. CHEATHAM, Congressional Clearinghouse on the Future, 722 House Annex, Washington DC 20515, USA. Publishes newsletter "What's Next?". Arranges dialogues on America's future between members of Congress and distinguished thinkers including E. F. Schumacher, Hazel Henderson, Alvin Toffler, Willis Harman. Keeps a "talent bank" of expert advisers on various aspects of the future.

ELIZABETH AND DAVID DODSON GRAY, The Bolton Institute, Suite 302, 1835 K Street NW, Washington DC 20006, USA. Matching the requirements of human societies with the welfare of natural systems. Recent papers include "The Grief Dimensions of the Transition from Growth to Material Equilibrium".

W. A. DYSON, Executive Director, Vanier Institute of the Family, 151 Slater, Ottawa K1P 5HS, Ontario, Canada. Developing a public policy framework which will promote social co-operation and the wellbeing of families and persons. Research and policy proposals, conferences and seminars, publications. Learning, family life, relationships, lifestyles, working and earning, the effect of the media, are among the subjects covered.

EILEEN EGAN, Catholic Relief Services, 1011 First Avenue, New York, NY, USA. Peace, disarmament, war resistance, non-violence.

ENVIRONMENTALISTS FOR FULL EMPLOYMENT, 1785 Massachusetts Avenue NW, Washington DC 20036, USA. (Richard Grossman). Publications include "Jobs and Energy" — an alternative approach which will provide safe energy, prosperity and jobs.

PETER GILLINGHAM, Intermediate Technology, 556 Santa Cruz Avenue, Menlo Park, California 94025, USA. Sponsor of important tours of the United States by E. F. Schumacher. Publishes regular reports. Network centre for intermediate, appropriate, alternative technology.

WILLIS W. HARMAN, Stanford Research Institute, Menlo Park, California, USA. Directs the Center for the Study of Social Policy at Stanford. Author of "An Incomplete Guide to the Future".[4] Engineering, alternative futures, educational policy, humanistic psychology.

HAZEL AND CARTER HENDERSON, Princeton Center for Alternative Futures, 60 Hodge Road, Princeton, New Jersey 08540, USA. Alternative futures, technology assessment, the coming economic transition, citizen power in the overdeveloped countries, the entropy state, etc., etc. An important network centre.

INSTITUTE FOR LOCAL SELF-RELIANCE, 1717 18th Street NW, Washington DC 20009, USA (Kathleen Fisher). Research and consultancy on how high density population areas can become independent and self-reliant. New technologies, institutions and small scale production systems. Newsletter "Self-Reliance".

BYRON KENNARD, 1785 Massachusetts Avenue NW, Room 212, Washington DC 20036, USA. National Council for Public Assessment of Technology, Environmentalists for Full Employment, voluntary networks and community organisations.

BERIT LAKEY, 4719 Springfield Avenue, Philadelphia, Pa. 19143, USA. Philadelphia Life Center (Movement for a New Society) —

a multi-generational support community for people involved in fundamental social change — "Moving Towards A New Society".[79]

JOHN McCLAUGHRY, Institute for Liberty and Community, Concord, Vermont 05824, USA. Concerned with the possibilities for a smallness coalition and for decentralising government, energy, economy, education, environmental protection and public finance in Vermont.

MICHAEL MARIEN, Information for Policy Design, 5413 Webster Road, LaFayette, NY 13084, USA. Author and publisher of "Societal Directions and Alternatives".[1] Literature and ideas about alternative futures and decentralist philosophies and politics.

DAVID MILLER, DCM Associates, 908 Fox Plaza, San Francisco, California 94102, USA. Futures study as an aspect of education. "Hopes and Fears Switchboard" — a do-it-yourself futures studies kit.

NEW ALCHEMY INSTITUTE, Box 432, Woods Hole, Mass. 02543, USA. (John and Nancy Todd). Practical research and education on behalf of humanity and the planet. Development of ecologically derived forms of energy, agriculture, aquaculture, housing and landscapes. Journal.

HENRYK SKOLIMOWSKI. Professor of Philosophy, Dept. of Humanities, University of Michigan, 525 East University, Ann Arbor, Michigan 48109, USA. Alternative futures. Alternatives in higher education. New environmental philosophy. Author of "Ecological Humanism".[78]

CATHY STARRS, The Public Policy Concern, Room 600, 71 Bank Street, Ottawa, Ontario K1P 5N2, Canada. Author of "Reworking the World: A Report on Changing Concepts of Work",[47] and of "Conversations with Canadians about the Future".

ALICE TEPPER MARLIN, Council on Economic Priorities, 84 5th Avenue, New York, NY 10011, USA. CEP examines the social performance and practices of business in such areas as equal employment, environmental impact, consumer health and safety, foreign investment, political influence, and military production. Studies, reports, newsletters.

JOHN TEPPER MARLIN, Council on Municipal Performance, 84 5th Avenue, New York, NY 10011, USA. COMP analyses and compares the performance of different cities in fields such as crime, housing, economic policies, pollution, health services, education, etc. Studies and Municipal Performance Reports are published.

ROBERT THEOBALD, PO Box 2240, Wickenburg, Arizona 85358, USA. Author of several books about the future, including "Beyond Despair: Directions for America's Third Century". Communications. Networks.

WILLIAM IRWIN THOMPSON, The Lindisfarne Association, 47 West 20th Street, New York, NY 10011, USA. "Humanity is in a period of profound evolutionary transformation. The members of Lindisfarne see technological civilisation becoming miniaturised and surrounded by a consciousness no longer polarised between mind and body, conscious and unconscious, male and female, spirit and matter." Lectures, seminars, tapes, books, newsletters.

ALVIN TOFFLER, 40 East 78th Street, New York, NY 10021, USA. Author of "Future Shock",[74] "The Eco-spasm Report", etc. Initiator of the "anticipatory democracy" movement — people participating in planning the future.

WORLD WATCH INSTITUTE, 1776 Massachusetts, Avenue NW, Washington DC 20036, USA. (Lester Brown — President). Interdisciplinary research and publications on global problems and social trends — including energy, food, women in politics, population, etc.

Europe*

FONDATION INTERNATIONALE DE L'INNOVATION SOCIALE, 20 Rue Laffitte, 75009 Paris, France. (Georges and Jeanine Gueron). Theory, concepts, applications and achievements of social innovation. Small communities, complexity, business enterprises, social fiction, exhibitions of social innovation. Conferences.

FUTURIBLES, 10 Rue Cernischi, 75017 Paris, France. (Hugues de Jouvenel). Centre of information about futures studies. Sponsors research on the future of society, changing lifestyles, and social progress. Library, reference service, conferences, publications.

ROBERT JUNGK, c/o Thames & Hudson, 30 Bloomsbury Street, London WC1B 3QP. Author of "The Everyman Project".[70] Alter-

---

* I am now able to amplify this short European list, with the addition of many new individuals and organisations.

native futures. Social inventions and social innovations. Participative "workshops" about the future.

BOB AND HEIDI WELKE, Zietenring 7, D-6200 Wiesbaden, West Germany. Network Quodlibeta — decentralist, anthropological, English language but continental Europe (as well as Britain and North America) in coverage.

Bibliography and References

A short list for suggested reading has been given at the end of each chapter except Chapter 5. The following is a list of publications to which reference has been made in the text.

1 Michael Marien: "Societal Directions and Alternatives": Information For Policy Design (Lafayette, New York 13084, USA), 1976.

2 Stanford Research Institute: "Alternative Futures For Environmental Policy Planning: 1975-2000": for the Environmental Protection Agency: National Technical Information Service (Springfield, Virginia 22151, USA), 1975.

3 James Robertson: "Power, Money and Sex: Towards A New Social Balance": Marion Boyars Publishers Ltd., (18 Brewer Street, London W1A 4AS), 1976.

4 Willis W. Harman: "An Incomplete Guide To The Future": The Portable Stanford (Stanford Alumni Association, Stanford, California, USA), 1976.

5 Robin Clarke: "Notes For The Future": Thames and Hudson, London, 1975.

6 Dennis Meadows et al.: "The Limits To Growth": Universe Books, New York, 1972.

7 M. Mesarovic and E. Pestel: "Mankind At The Turning Point": Hutchinson, London, 1975.

8 Ronald Higgins: "The Seventh Enemy": The Observer, London, 1975.

9 Robert L. Heilbroner: "An Inquiry Into The Human Prospect": Calder and Boyars, London, 1975.

10 The Ecologist: "Blueprint For Survival": Penguin Books, London, 1972.

11 Conservation Society: Annual Report for 1976: Conservation Society (see appendix), 1976.

12 Herman E. Daly (ed.): "Toward A Steady-State Economy": Freeman, San Francisco, 1973.

13 Herman Kahn et al.: "The Next 200 Years": Associated Business Programmes, London, 1977.

14 Daniel Bell: "The Coming Of Post-Industrial Society": Penguin Books, London, 1976.

15 Robert L. Heilbroner: "Business Civilisation in Decline":

Marion Boyars, London, 1976.

16 William Irwin Thompson: "Evil And World Order": Harper and Row, New York, 1976.

17 L. S. Stavrianos: "The Promise Of The Coming Dark Age": Freeman, San Francisco, 1976.

18 Murray Bookchin: "Post Scarcity Anarchism": Wildwood House, London, 1974.

19 R. H. Tawney: "Religion And The Rise Of Capitalism": Penguin, London, 1938.

20 Gurth Higgin: "Scarcity, Abundance And Depletion: The Challenge To Continuing Management Education": Inaugural Lecture, Loughborough University of Technology, 1975.

21 Axel Leijonhufvud: "On Keynesian Economics And The Economics Of Keynes": Oxford, 1968.

22 Edith Simon: "The Saints": Penguin Books, London, 1972.

23 George C. Lodge: "The New American Ideology": Knopf, New York, 1976.

24 E. F. Schumacher: "Small Is Beautiful: A Study Of Economics As If People Mattered": Blond and Briggs, London, 1973. (E. F. Schumacher's later book, "A Guide For The Perplexed", Jonathan Cape, London, 1977, was published as this book went to the printers.)

25 Martin Pfaff (ed.): "Frontiers Of Social Thought": North Holland Publishing Co., 1976.

26 Fred Hirsch: "Social Limits To Growth": Routledge and Kegan Paul, London, 1977.

27 Peter Jay: "Employment, Inflation and Politics": Institute of Economic Affairs, Occasional Paper 46, London, 1976.

28 Hazel Henderson: "Citizen Power in the Overdeveloped Countries": World Issues, December 1976/January 1977, the Center for the Study of Democratic Institutions, Santa Barbara, California 93103, USA.

29 Peter Draper: "The Unhealthy Economy: A Physician's View": The Lancet, October 30, 1976.

30 Hugh Stretton: "Housing and Government": Australian Broadcasting Commission, Sydney, 1974.

31 Tom Forester: "Do the British sincerely want to be rich?": New Society, April 28, 1977.

32 Abraham H. Maslow: "Motivation and Personality": 2nd edition, Harper and Row, 1970.

33 James Robertson: "Profit Or People? The New Social Role Of Money": Calder and Boyars, London, 1974.

34 S. J. Prais: "The Evolution Of Giant Firms In Britain": Cambridge University Press, 1976.

35 Report of the Committee of Enquiry under Lord Bullock's chairmanship on "Industrial Democracy": HMSO, Cmnd. 6706, 1977.

36 Report No. 2 of the Royal Commission on the "Distribution of Income And Wealth" under Lord Diamond's chairmanship: HMSO, Cmnd. 6172, 1975.

37 John Morris: "Managerial Effectiveness: The Problem Of A Paradigm": an unpublished paper sent privately to the author.

38 Peter Drucker: "The Unseen Revolution: How Pension Fund Socialism Came To America": Harper and Row, New York, 1976.

39 For example, J. K. Galbraith: "The New Industrial State", Pelican Books, 1969.

40 Norman Macrae: "The Coming Entrepreneurial Revolution": The Economist, London, December 25, 1976.

41 T. S. Kuhn: "The Structure Of Scientific Revolutions": University of Chicago Press, 1970.

42 Tom Burke: "The New Wealth": Unpublished paper, 1977.

43 Boston Women's Health Book Collective: "Our Bodies Ourselves": Simon and Schuster, New York, 1976.

44 Peter Cadogan: "Direct Democracy": 1 Hampstead Hill Gardens, London NW3, 1975.

45 Ciaran McKeown: "The Price of Peace": Belfast, 1976. (See appendix — Peace People.)

46 Aurelio Peccei: "The Human Quality": Pergamon, 1977.

47 Gail Stewart and Cathy Starrs: 'Reworking The World: A Report On Changing Concepts Of Work": Ottawa, 1973.

48 See Mike Cooley in "Undercurrents 20" (February/March 1977).

49 "Employment, Growth And Basic Needs: A One-World Problem": International Labour Office (ILO), Geneva, 1976.

50 David Elliott: "The Future of Work": Open University Press, 1975.

51 David Elliott and Ruth Elliott: "The Control Of Technology": Wykeham Publications, 1976.

52 Colin Hutchinson: "The Crisis Of Lifestyles": Conservation Society, 1975.

53 Gregory Bateson: "Steps To An Ecology Of Mind": Paladin, 1973.

54   Raimundo Panikkar: "Myth In Religious Phenomenology":
      Monchanin, Montreal, June/December 1975.
55   Ivan D. Illich: "Tools For Conviviality": Calder and Boyars,
      1973.
56   "The Serving Professions?": Vanier Institute of the Family,
      Ottawa, 1974.
57   John Southgate and Rosemary Randall: "The Barefoot Psycho-
      analyst": Association of Karen Horney Psychoanalytic Coun-
      sellors, 1976.
58   Various publications from the Manager (Public Affairs), Royal
      Bank of Canada, Montreal.
59   John Turner: "Housing By People": Marion Boyars Pub-
      lishers, London, 1976.
60   Alice Coleman: "Is Planning Really Necessary": Royal Geo-
      graphical Society, London, May 1976.
61   John G. U. Adams: "You're Never Alone With Schizophrenia":
      Industrial Marketing Management 4, 1972.
62   Abraham Maslow: "Towards A Psychology Of Being": Van
      Nostrand Reinhold, 1968.
63   Sir James Robertson: "Transition In Africa": Hurst, London,
      1974.
64   Peter Mathias: "The First Industrial Nation": Methuen,
      London, 1969.
65   Stephen Verney: "Into The New Age": Fontana, 1976.
66   Gurth Higgin: "Symptoms Of Tomorrow": Plume Press/
      Ward Lock, 1973.
67   Eric Berne: "Games People Play": Grove Press, New York,
      1964.
68   Michael Maccoby: "The Gamesman": Simon and Schuster,
      New York, 1976.
69   Bryan Clarke: "The Causes Of Biological Diversity": Scien-
      tific American, August 1975.
70   Robert Jungk: "The Everyman Project": Thames and Hudson,
      London, 1976.
71   Ivan Illich: "Deschooling Society": Calder and Boyars, Lon-
      don, 1971.
72   Ivan Illich: "Medical Nemesis": Calder and Boyars, London,
      1975.
73   Ivan Illich et al.: "Disabling Professions": Marion Boyars,
      London, 1977.
74   Alvin Toffler: "Future Shock": Bodley Head, 1970.
75   Charles Hampden-Turner: "Sane Asylum": Morrow, New

York, 1977.
76 Peter Abbs and Graham Carey: "Proposal For A New College": Heinemann Educational Books, London, 1977.
77 Peter Chapman: "Fuel's Paradise": Penguin, 1975.
78 Henryk Skolimowski: "Ecological Humanism": Tract Nos. 19 and 20 (see appendix — Peter Abbs).
79 Gowan, Lakey, Moyer and Taylor: "Moving Toward A New Society": Movement For A New Society, 1976 (see appendix — Berit Lakey).
80 "Learning For Change In World Society": World Studies Project, 24 Palace Chambers, Bridge Street, London SW1.
81 Patrick Rivers: "Living Better On Less": Turnstone Books, London, 1977.